Attracting Prosperity through the Chakras

Attracting Prosperity through the Chakras

Cyndi Dale

THE CROSSING PRESS
Berkeley | Toronto

The Crossing Press
A division of Ten Speed Press
P.O. Box 7123
Berkeley, California 94707
www.tenspeed.com

Distributed in Australia by Simon and Schuster Australia, in Canada by Ten Speed Press Canada, in New Zealand by Southern Publishers Group, in South Africa by Real Books, and in the United Kingdom and Europe by Airlift Book Company.

Cover design by Lisa Buckley
Interior design by Rachel Holscher

Library of Congress Cataloging-in-Publication Data is on file with the publisher

ISBN 1-58091-162-5

Previously published in 2003 under the title *Making and Managing Money Through the Chakras* (ISBN 1-59298-034-1)

Printed in the U.S.A.

1 2 3 4 5 6 7 — 07 06 05 04

Dedicated to the following incredible people

Foremost, my thanks to Pam Curran and Peter Watson for sharing their abundant intelligence, wit, support, and understanding of the legal aspects of financial safety. They truly understand the meaning of giving, and this book is dedicated to them.

And special recognition to Wendy Kardia and Ruth Noack for upholding the household and business aspects of my life so I could write; Cathy Scofield for her invaluable editing and listening skills; Lilia Toftoul, my partner and agent in playing in the world; J. J. Jeska for her energy and nerve; and my mother, Solveig Norstog, for being the mom.

Contents

Introduction:
Your Personal Doorway to Success

Do you know that the key to financial success is already in your hands? It doesn't matter whether your pockets are full of gold— or moths. For the key to work, however, you have to open the right door: your own personal doorway to success. To find your doorway, you have to use the right map.

No two individuals think, act, or even eat the same way. So why should everyone make money the same way? The color of your eyes is coded in the intricate strands of DNA in every one of your cells. Your personality is the outcome of a complex weaving of genetics, upbringing, and a little something special, whether you call it kismet, fate, or soul. Your moneymaking and management style, however, is carried in a set of energy genetics— your chakras.

You won't spot the word "chakra" in a corporate annual report or in most books about investment and wealth, or find it covered by dry and worldly topics like money, savings, debt-to-income ratios, PEs, investments, wealth, and finances.

A chakra is an invisible yet very real part of your body. Unlike your liver and heart, your chakras can only be seen with special equipment and measurement tools. But they are real, as real as energy and love and potential success.

Chakras are energy organs. There are hundreds of them. The most important chakras, however, are the eleven chakras that govern your daily life and actions. These chakras convert spiritual energy into physical matter and back again. They can seize a physical disease and transform it into energy to burn. They can also take your ideas about money and spin them into gold.

Everyone is equipped with chakras. Some of your chakras are more developed than other chakras and some are weaker. By amplifying your strongest chakras, you can accentuate your financial strengths. You can figure out your moneymaking gifts, learn how to evaluate investment opportunities, make smart and personalized money decisions, and deal with and avert financial disasters. In short, by working with your chakras, you can skip the need to be born with a "silver spoon" and dig for the treasure that's already yours! Want to learn more? Then open your door to personal success!

Money, Money Everywhere, and Where Is Yours When the Bills Come In?

"And so they went on, like a caravan of exhausted minstrels in motley browns and greys: Francis, Teige, and Tomas all walking ahead and trying each in his own way to imagine a future that might repair the past."[1]

MONEY WORRIES

You might be satisfied with your current financial success. But I doubt it. Even the wealthiest individual has money concerns, as do those of us whose idea of stretching the paycheck snaps it in two. We all ask ourselves questions like these:

- How can I make more money?
- How can I make wiser investment decisions?
- How can I save money when it's so hard to make ends meet?
- How can I make money and still spend time with loved ones?
- Can I make money without sacrificing my values?
- Is it possible to really do what I love to do—and still make money?
- What are the best ways to manage the money I do have?
- How can I get out of—or prevent—debt? Or financial disaster?
- How can I become wealthier—and happier—with the money I do have?

Fortunately or unfortunately, money is the commodity that measures security. All of us need and use money to survive because very few things in life are free. Even a smile from your child has a debt-to-delivery ratio. Have you added up the price of toothpaste, dental bills, and orthodontia? I don't think most of us really want to know the actual cost of a smile or of life itself. Whether your annual budget has three or ten zeros behind it, chances are good that you worry about money.

As a culture, we worry about the money that we have, asking ourselves if we have enough, if our savings are safe, or if our investments are plunging below the waistline. We fret even more about money that we don't have—especially, how to get it!

Much of the time, we worry because it has been hard to make and manage money. Obscured in the past are our financial difficulties, each protesting temporary burial. We might achieve success, but don't we always wonder when failure will return? We don't even trust the achievements we gain!

We can't change the past. We can act in the present, but not if we're worrying about the future. When we worry, we only create more worries and lose the energy we need to act efficiently and effectively.

What if you could take all that energy going into worrying and actually make more money with it? What if you could take all the failures and worries of the past and use that energy to build a new structure for the future? What if all that extra and wasted energy could go into purchasing more financial success—and with it, more joy and fun? It's possible. In fact, it's more than possible. *It's promised.*

THE PROMISE OF FINANCIAL SECURITY

Every spiritual tradition promises that our needs will be met, assuming the presence of a loving consciousness or being of Spirit that assures our provisions and true desires. Whether you call this being God, the Source, the Divine, Christ, the Goddess, the Great Spirit, the Almighty, the Buddha, the Krishna, the Holy Spirit, or the White Light, this being of unconditional love quite simply wants the best for you.

As Jesus says in the Christian New Testament:

"Consider the ravens: They do not sow or reap, they have no storeroom or barn; yet God feeds them. And how much more valuable you are than birds!" (Luke 12: 24)

"But seek his kingdom, and these things will be given to you as well." (Luke 12: 31)

We are promised the necessities of life, indeed even affluence, with one caveat: "Seek the kingdom." This is not a religious undertaking. Seeking is a spiritual journey, one involving the full expression of your innate, divinely bestowed gifts and spiritual purpose. Your spiritual journey begins and ends with the acknowledgment and expression of the spirit within you.

From a Taoist point of view, the spirit entering flesh is "graceful instead of abrupt, flowing rather than hesitant, it is infinitely generous."[2] When you think, feel, and act from your spiritual core, you naturally become more generous toward others, who in turn generate care toward you. As you share your innate gifts, the world shares gifts with you, a worldview supported by Hinduism through the emphasis of work as a means to enlightenment. As the basis of the third path to God, which is called karma yoga, the key to living in the Divine through service is to "throw yourself into your work with everything you have, only do so wisely, in a way that will bring the highest rewards, not just trivia."[3]

When accomplished spiritually, making money is never trivial; rather, it is the outcome of pursuing your true work.

THE MATTER OF MONEY:
THE MATTER OF MAKING A DIFFERENCE

You are a vital and important person and are here on this planet at this time because the world needs you. You have work to do.

Owning your unique value connects you to the Divine and therefore the sources of prosperity. As shared by Cherokee wisewoman Dhyani Ywahoo, "We are shaping, like crystals, a field of mind. We live in a field of mind. We can call this Buddha mind, God mind, 'What It Is.' The Tsalagi say it is the Great Mystery, Ywahoo, 'that which is unmanifest and becoming and contains within it the seed of our potential.'"[4]

You are a seed of divine potential. You are an emissary of the Divine, here on this planet to achieve a special assignment, to carry out a spiritual destiny that will change the world. Your destiny involves expressing, experiencing, and embodying at least one spiritual truth throughout all of life. As you live this truth, you become it. What you become then returns to you.

A spiritual truth differs from an everyday truth in that it involves higher concepts like love, justice, faith, honesty, joy, healing, and integrity. While thousands of individuals might all seek to express the same spiritual truth, each will do so in a different and vital way.

For instance, you and your neighbor might both be concerned with embracing and teaching the spiritual truth of honesty. She might be especially gifted at articulating honesty through words, while you reflect honesty through action. To carry your truth into the world, you are equipped with the gifts, attributes, and traits that will allow you to act with integrity in work, relationships, and leisure. Your neighbor will bear different gifts and characteristics. She might be more skilled at writing or speaking. Neither of you are more or less gifted than the other; you are both perfectly equipped to perform your particular purpose.

Your spiritual purpose is programmed into every cell of your body and every fiber of your being. The gifts supporting your purpose are encoded within you as well. Certainly, some of them are replicated from your physical genetics. You can inherit the tendency to be musical, athletic, or intelligent. But the spiritually oriented gifts, those which directly feed your spiritual purpose, are preset into a masterful and powerful part of you called your energy system—as is your moneymaking ability. As long as you do what you're spiritually called to do, you'll make money. You see, making and managing money is simply doing what matters, and then the money that matters is energized to you.

Exercise: Doing What Matters

For one day, decide to do only what really matters to you. Does it matter if you go to the bank or pick up the clothes? Hug your child or make dinner? Does one attitude matter more than another? Concentrate on doing only what really matters inside of you and at the end of the day, think about these questions:

1. What did I learn about what is important to me?
2. How did I feel when I did what matters?
3. How do I seem to matter to others?
4. What difference do I think I make in the world?

2

The Energy of Prosperity

*Says Merlin: "We are almost entirely void
and would easily pass through the ground and
each other like clouds if not for the electrostatic force
in the enormous spaces between the atoms. It is that
force that Camelot is designed to work upon."*[5]

IT'S ALL ENERGY

Everything in the world is made of energy, from a thought to a plant to—yes, money! When we're sick, we feel "low energy." When we're excited, we say that we have "high energy." If you attract and emanate the "right" energy, you help turn the world into Camelot, or the Kingdom of Heaven. You'll also increase your moneymaking potential.

Let's consider how energy works, and you'll have a better idea of what I'm talking about.

There are many, many types of energies but they all reduce to two major categories: fast and slow moving energy. Fast moving energy travels faster than the speed of light and is able to convey information, ideas, healing, and knowledge instantly. Slow moving energy treks like a backpacker loaded down with camping goods. Slow moving energy goes slower than the speed of light. You can still receive all the supplies you need, but it will take a little longer.

Fast moving energy could also be called tachyon, psychic, or spiritual energy, while slow moving energy could also be labeled quark, material, or physical energy. There are many differences between tachyons and quarks but the primary one is that tachyons, named after a certain type of subatomic particle, don't have to obey the traffic cops of the natural universe. A tachyon particle can give you a thought before you've thought it or return with a prayer answered before you've prayed. Quarks, on the other hand, are law abiding. A quark particle must bend toward gravity, stop at stop signs, and linger in the crossroads until other traffic has passed. If you want fast change (or quick abundance), you want to marshal tachyons rather than quarks.

How do these energy particles know what to do? All energy contains information. Each and every particle, person, or object is fashioned from energy programmed with information that tells other energies how to respond. You might know a hot plate is hot because you just stuck it in the oven. That's called common sense. You might also decipher the message because you see steam rising off the plate. Now, you're reading the "slow" or quark energy about the plate. The energy emitting from the plate, however, sends its own message. The fast-moving energy in the plate is broadcasting its own communication as the tachyons psychically state, "The plate is hot." That's how you "intuitively" know that one plate is hotter than the others, that is, if you're paying attention to your intuition, the part of you that can decipher fast-moving "information-energy."

By putting intuition and common sense together, you can learn how to interpret incoming tachyon messages about money-making ventures and send tachyon messages that will increase abundance. Sure, you can keep going the slow hard way. And you'll still have to do a fair amount of everyday, routine work no matter what. Want a job? You might still have to peruse the want ads, interview through an agency, and network with friends. That's the "quark path" to fame and fortune. But you can also upgrade your process by managing your tachyon or spiritual energy. You can attract a certain amount of fame and fortune—as long as you do it the right way, the way that fits your spiritual path and purpose.

But Can You Energize Money?

Let's say you need a job. You can print resumes and distribute them, working the quark way to convince others that you're a good job candidate. Someone might believe you and hire you. Then again, maybe not. Want to energize the process? Make sure your tachyon messages are in line with your desires. That way, others' subconscious will do the work for you. Rather than reading your resume, they'll be able to read your energy.

You're going to be more successful at anything you do if you're expressing the message that you're capable and able. If you hold a positive viewpoint of yourself, your information-energy will reflect this attitude and the people around you will respond. They will like you, see you as successful, and help you become more successful.

Now, the opposite can also be true. You might not like yourself. You might think you don't deserve to be financially stable. Consequently, the invisible messages you broadcast will tell people to avoid you. You certainly won't get any great job offers!

Your spirit is the most vital and animate part of yourself. In fact, it's your "real self." If you're expressing your spiritual purpose and personality, people will enthusiastically assist you. You will emit tachyon, or invisible, messages that others will intuitively read and respect.

Do you want to make money faster? Hold onto it longer? Multiply your abundance? Enjoy your moneymaking endeavors? By working from your spiritual purpose, you can access the spiritual or fast-moving energy available for success. While other people are waiting for money to grow on trees, you might be able to "snap" your finger—and presto! Well, maybe not quite that quick. You will feel happy about the money that you do make, however, and energized to make more.

Ready to use your key to personal success? The doorways lie within. They are called your chakras.

YOUR ENERGY SYSTEM: DOORWAYS TO PROSPERITY

Your chakras are your individualized doorways to success. You have hundreds of chakras, spinning wheels of light that convert tachyons into quarks and quarks into tachyons. These energy centers or organs, as they are called, are central to abundance. Through your chakras, you can take an idea and make it real, and take a problem and make it disappear. Even more important, your chakras are coded for your personal destiny. By understanding what lies within your chakras, you can uncover your spiritual destiny and extraordinary moneymaking abilities.

Chakras are part of a larger framework called the energy system. Your energy system is a highly complex set of energy bodies that accesses both spiritual and physical energies. Each energy body is like a light prism. It catches white light and divides it into various rainbow colors, then merges this myriad into a single tractor beam again. Through the energy bodies, you can access larger spiritual forces and focus them on a specific goal. You can also break a problem into its component parts and better tackle a difficult situation.

You can see why accessing an energy organ such as one of your strongest, most developed chakras can help create success. Why not read the information of the universe? Why not tell the world and the people in it how to better respond to you?

GETTING TO THE GOLD:
YOUR PERSONAL ENERGY SYSTEM

While there are thousands of energy bodies and hundreds of chakras, you can accomplish most of your goals working with the eleven major chakras. In addition, it's helpful to understand the eleven main auric fields paired with each chakra. These eleven brother-sister energy centers help regulate just about everything in your life, from spiritual purpose to money. While everyone has the same chakras and auric fields, they work differently in each person. Understanding your own unique energy blueprint can help you materialize your spiritual purpose and abundance.

To better understand how your energy system works, picture yourself without clothes for a minute. Now imagine a vast set of conical circles emanating from or in alignment with your spine. These are your chakras. Each chakra has a different physical, emotional, mental, and spiritual function and connects with a different set of physical organs. Notice that your chakras don't stop at the skin. Their multihued energies flow into another set of energies that surround your body. These individualized bands of colors are your auric fields. These also regulate various physical, emotional, mental, and spiritual functions. In that each chakra is paired with a specific auric field, the chakras and energy centers work together to keep you safe, secure, and able to express yourself through all that you do.

Science is proving the reality of these energy centers. You can read more about this scientific research in my other books. While it's affirming to have science substantiate these energy centers, knowledge of the chakras and auric fields is as old as humanity.

Long ago, our ancestors diagnosed problems and illnesses and provided solutions to life's predicaments by working with the energy system. By peering into the chakras, healers of old pinpointed the causes of illness and issues. By energizing the right chakras and auric fields, these same wise people helped individuals transform their lives for increased health, prosperity, and loving relationships.

Our ancestors understood the power of energy. They knew that these invisible, swirling units of light were doorways into prosperity.

What worked yesterday can certainly work today.

What most modern mystics don't know is that you can read much, much more than someone's physical, emotional, or even mental well-being in the energy system. Your chakras and their corresponding auric fields hold the "energetic genetics" of your spiritual purpose, basic nature, intuitive skills, value system, workplace focus, decision-making style, moneymaking and management style, and much, much more. Your energy centers and mine might be as similar as one computer hardware system is to another. But our software is different. By accessing and analyzing your personal energy system, you can determine your basic nature and therefore your personal keys to financial abundance.

One of the easiest ways to uncover this energetic information is to figure out your strongest or most developed energy centers. You will be stronger and more gifted in certain centers than I will be. After all, you and I are called to very different life goals. I might need one specific set of characteristics or tendencies but not others. Based on my spiritual purpose, then, one or more energy centers, each containing a set of gifts, tendencies, and traits, will be more potent than others.

Basically, you need the strength of certain energy centers more than others to accomplish your destiny. From a spiritual viewpoint, money is just a means to an end. It is a supportive mechanism for meeting your spiritual goals. But it is also a necessary tool to achieve success in the real world. Encapsulated into your energy system and your strongest energy centers are the tools you need to be as prosperous and financially successful as you are destined to become. Figure out your strongest energy centers and you can then figure out how to make the financial decisions you need to make to be affluent and happy.

Quiz: Your Strongest Chakras

There are a lot of books about spiritual purpose and numerous tests, quizzes, and processes to help you uncover your vocational calling. Few help you unlock your spiritual nature and then continue to help you figure out your spiritually based money style. This quiz, "Your Strongest Chakras," is designed to pinpoint your strongest versus weakest chakras so you can better understand your personal destiny and your moneymaking style.

Directions: Please circle your responses to the following questions, asking yourself if you agree or disagree with the statement. The scale is 0 to 5. Zero means "I disagree completely," while five means "I agree completely." You will score the quiz after taking it and work with it in the next chapters, so save your results.

1. I would consider myself a physical person in that I am active and like to exercise.

   0   1   2   3   4   5

2. My feelings often tell me what's important in my life.

   0   1   2   3   4   5

3. Love is more important than money; money is only useful when it's helping others.

   0   1   2   3   4   5

4. I consider myself a mystic in that things magical or supernatural fascinate me.

0 1 2 3 4 5

5. It's more important to me to be creative than to make or save money.

0 1 2 3 4 5

6. I need to speak or write my financial goals to make them happen.

0 1 2 3 4 5

7. Before I can make a decision, I must pray or meditate about it.

0 1 2 3 4 5

8. I consider myself an idealist because I believe that only ideals are important.

0 1 2 3 4 5

9. I'm happiest when I buy something solid and tangible with money.

0 1 2 3 4 5

10. I consider myself a visual person in that I can picture ideas, needs, and desires in my head.

0 1 2 3 4 5

11. I would only invest in a product or company that is run in business-like fashion and can account for every penny.

0 1 2 3 4 5

12. I would like to be a healer, if that means helping people become more loving in one way or another.

0 1 2 3 4 5

13. I think I should be able to command money to appear out of the air.

0 1 2 3 4 5

14. Plain and simple, money is power.

0 1 2 3 4 5

15. I would spend any amount of money on a hurt animal.

0 1 2 3 4 5

16. I would like to perform miracles whenever I want to do so.

0 1 2 3 4 5

17. I would be open to verbally hear guidance from the invisible realm, such as from angels or the deceased.

0 1 2 3 4 5

18. I need to imagine or visualize a goal before I can work for it.

0 1 2 3 4 5

19. I am a spiritual person in that my spiritual life is more important than anything else.

0 1 2 3 4 5

20. I would consider myself a feelings-based person in that I feel all my feelings deeply.

0 1 2 3 4 5

21. I like to think that everything in life works toward a higher ideal.

0 1 2 3 4 5

22. I can't stand it when a plant or animal is hurt.

0 1 2 3 4 5

23. I would consider myself a relational person in that I am always aware of my own and others' relationship needs and problems.

0 1 2 3 4 5

24. I would consider myself a thinking-based person in that it's important to gather and analyze the data before making a decision.

0 1 2 3 4 5

25. To make a difference in the world, you need to produce a service or a product that is useful, tangible, and practical.

0 1 2 3 4 5

26. I believe that there are other worlds, planes, and dimensions and I want to be a connecting point between them.

0 1 2 3 4 5

27. I believe the main goal of making money is to take care of other people, especially my loved ones.

0 1 2 3 4 5

28. I usually make decisions based on logic and analysis.

0 1 2 3 4 5

29. I would consider myself a communicative person in that I love to share and hear what others have to say.

0 1 2 3 4 5

30. I could never spend money on anything that would damage the environment.

0 1 2 3 4 5

31. Money is only useful if it furthers the Divine plan.

0 1 2 3 4 5

32. I can sometimes sense the presence of invisible spirits or God's own Spirit.

0 1 2 3 4 5

33. I would like to transform any negative situation into something positive with my own will.

    0   1   2   3   4   5

34. Sometimes, I feel others' feelings as if they are my own.

    0   1   2   3   4   5

35. I believe that there are patterns to life, reasons that certain people come together or not.

    0   1   2   3   4   5

36. I can't do checkbooks; I only understand money if I can hold it in my hands.

    0   1   2   3   4   5

37. I believe the safest investments are the most tangible, such as in durable goods, real estate, property, or anything that you can "touch."

    0   1   2   3   4   5

38. I like to constantly read or hear about how my investments are doing.

    0   1   2   3   4   5

39. Making money is a long-range objective: I can put up with short-term fluctuations for long-term gain.

    0   1   2   3   4   5

40. Living an ethical life that supports my value system is more important than having money.

    0   1   2   3   4   5

41. I like to invest my money in endeavors that are logical, intelligently explained, and well organized.

    0   1   2   3   4   5

42. Before I can make or invest money, I need to create a long-range plan.

    0   1   2   3   4   5

43. I know what's right by how my body reacts; for instance, I'll get a physical reaction when I either like or don't like someone.

0   1   2   3   4   5

44. I'm like a lightning bolt; I leave a mark through humor or by saying something pointed, unusual, or sarcastic.

0   1   2   3   4   5

45. Good and bad, like black and white, aren't always what they seem; I can tell the real difference, no matter what others think or say.

0   1   2   3   4   5

46. There is no such thing as "bad" or "blood" money; you can change the properties of any substance at will.

0   1   2   3   4   5

47. I like to invest my money in creative endeavors, either my own or someone else's.

0   1   2   3   4   5

48. When I die, I want to give all my money to a cause, like world peace or solving world hunger.

0   1   2   3   4   5

49. I like to budget and manage my money logically.

0   1   2   3   4   5

50. I put relationship needs before money.

0   1   2   3   4   5

51. I often convert my thoughts into pictures.

0   1   2   3   4   5

52. I like to make something creative with my time and money.

0   1   2   3   4   5

53. I'm happier in nature than anywhere else.

    0   1   2   3   4   5

54. I trust my ability to analyze and go by my "gut sense" to make the right decisions.

    0   1   2   3   4   5

55. Making money is vital to being successful and feeling accomplished.

    0   1   2   3   4   5

56. I love to spend money on books, music, and anything that helps me communicate with the outside world.

    0   1   2   3   4   5

57. If I had a million dollars to invest, I would make sure it's invested in companies that respect the environment.

    0   1   2   3   4   5

58. Money is only useful if it supports an ideal.

    0   1   2   3   4   5

59. I usually make decisions based on how my choices might affect relationships.

    0   1   2   3   4   5

60. I often see patterns in what is occurring around the world.

    0   1   2   3   4   5

61. You must be powerful to make a difference in this world, although you may have to change other worlds to make a difference here.

    0   1   2   3   4   5

62. People have always said that I'm a good communicator.

    0   1   2   3   4   5

63. I would like to use spiritual forces to get money when I want it.

0   1   2   3   4   5

64. I have to visualize an idea before I can understand it.

0   1   2   3   4   5

65. You should never surrender your value system to make money.

0   1   2   3   4   5

66. I believe I have the power and the right to change the weather when it's necessary.

0   1   2   3   4   5

Scoring: Please add up your scores in each of the following eleven categories. We will work with your final numbers in the next few chapters.

Category One:
1, 9, 25, 37, 43, 55

Category Two:
2, 5, 20, 34, 47, 52

Category Three:
11, 24, 28, 41, 49, 54

Category Four:
3, 12, 23, 27, 50, 59

Category Five:
6, 17, 29, 38, 56, 62

Category Six:
10, 18, 39, 42, 51, 64

Category Seven:
    7, 19, 31, 32, 40, 65

Category Eight:
    4, 14, 26, 44, 45, 61

Category Nine:
    8, 21, 35, 48, 58, 60

Category Ten:
    15, 22, 30, 36, 53, 57

Category Eleven:
    13, 16, 33, 46, 63, 66

Working Your Energy Gift Order

"Now to each one the manifestation of the Spirit is given for the common good. To one there is through the Spirit the message of wisdom, to another the message of knowledge by the same Spirit, to another faith by the same Spirit, to another gifts of healing by that one Spirit, to another miraculous powers, to another prophecy, to another distinguishing between spirits, to another speaking in different kinds of tongues, and to still another the interpretation of tongues."
(1 Corinthians 12: 7–10)

YOUR GIFTS

Your strongest and most developed chakras are vitalized for a reason. You need the gifts within them to actively express your spiritual purpose and to attract the financial abundance you need to achieve your destiny.

We're going to analyze the quiz "Your Strongest Chakras" to determine your strongest versus weakest chakras. Through this assessment, we are figuring out your energetic gift order.

Your energetic gift order outlines your chakras from strongest to weakest. Your strongest chakras contain the gifts and attributes most vital to your spiritual purpose; most of the time your weakest chakras are the least important in regard to accomplishing your spiritual goals.

Most individuals don't need eleven strong chakras. Different energy centers admit different energies. Your strongest and most developed chakras (and related auric fields) are activated to meet your spiritual destiny. Figuring out your strongest chakras helps you create a blueprint describing your personality, gifts—and moneymaking style. When we're done interpreting your strongest chakras, we'll use the same gift order lineup to analyze your moneymaking and management abilities.

YOUR ENERGY GIFT ORDER: FIGURING YOUR BASIC PERSONALITY AND SPIRITUAL NATURE

Most individuals have one to three strong energy centers. You will want to accentuate the gifts and styles found within these energy centers as you move from energy explanation into practical life management. You can figure out your entire gift order by ordering your quiz scores in order of highest to lowest scores. You will put tying scores next to each other. The highest possible score is 30 points and the lowest is 0. When tabulating your categories, know that each category represents a different chakra/auric field pair. I'll stick with indicating the corresponding chakra, as chakras usually lead the auric field in potency.

My scores, for example, look like this.

Category One: 30
Category Two: 24
Category Three: 18
Category Four: 21
Category Five: 24
Category Six: 30
Category Seven: 18
Category Eight: 30
Category Nine: 09
Category Ten: 24
Category Eleven: 25

To obtain my full gift order, I am going to fill in the following box:

Gift Order Table

Place	Score	Category/Chakra

Here is an example of my own gift order table.

Gift Order Table

Place	Score	Category/Chakra
First place	30 points	1, 6, 8
Second place	25 points	11
Third place	24 points	2, 5, 10
Fourth place	21 points	4
Fifth place	18 points	7, 3
Sixth place	9 points	9

By the time you've finished this part of the decoding, you have accounted for each of the eleven categories representing a different chakra/auric field. There aren't good or bad scores. I've seen the entire range. Some individuals have an outstanding single score and then a number of low scores. I've met someone with five top scores, all at 30 points! Scores are as personal as are individuals.

You're now ready to make a first cut at figuring out your personality and basic drives. Here is a quick run-down of what each chakra represents in relation to your spiritual nature.

THE BASIC CHAKRA STYLES

Chakra One:	Manifester
Chakra Two:	Feeler
Chakra Three:	Thinker
Chakra Four:	Relater
Chakra Five:	Communicator

Chakra Six:	Visionary
Chakra Seven:	Spiritualist
Chakra Eight:	Shaman
Chakra Nine:	Idealist
Chakra Ten:	Naturalist
Chakra Eleven:	Commander

We're going to examine each of these basic personality types so you can get a first read on your overall personality traits and spiritual nature. I'm also going to label your "chakra color." Each chakra is typically characterized by a specific color that represents the energetic frequency of the chakra in the body. Usually, the lower the chakra in the body, the closer it is to infrared versus ultraviolet hues. I'm also going to sketch the auric field accompanying each chakra so you can determine your other strengths and capabilities. Finally, I'm going to summarize the development sequence of each chakra. Each chakra activates at a certain age, during which time it locks in your responses to life experiences. This information will be helpful when you review your gift order to determine your moneymaking and management styles. Financial blocks are often incurred during a chakra's developmental years. If you clear the block, you can become more fiscally secure.

Chakra One: Manifester

You are the most primal and corporeal of all the chakra personality types. You are highly physical and like what the physical world has to offer. Your primary objective is to meet your own primary needs, especially as they relate to physical and material concerns, and then expand from there. You feel successful when you are able to build or create tangible resources for other people. Inevitably, your spiritual calling will propel you into bottom-line endeavors that lead to material success.

Chakra Color: Your color is RED.

First Auric Field: The first auric field enables you to attract material energy and deal with life in a physically active manner.

Chakra Development: This chakra is developed in-uterus through six months of age. You are therefore primarily impacted by issues of safety, security, worthiness, and deserving.

CHAKRA TWO: FEELER

You are the feeling-sensitive of the chakra universe. While others might think you too emotional, you prefer the word "expressive." Along with your need to feel deeply comes an innate creativity. You are driven to create something new, to leave a mark on the world never before seen. As you learn how to cope with your feeling-nature, you naturally develop compassion and mercy for others. Your sensuality, appreciation of beauty, and your feeling-expressiveness merge into a divine whole. No matter what, your spiritual purpose will call upon your ability to creatively convert feelings into artistry; whether you are a therapist or a graphic artist, you will convey compassion, symmetry, and mercy in all that you do.

Chakra Color: Your color is ORANGE.

Second Auric Field: The second auric field alerts you to others' feelings and your own emotional-based reaction to the world. You will always know what others are really feeling, no matter what they say or do.

Chakra Development: This chakra is developed from six months to 2½ years of age. You will be affected by the feelings of others, the need for community, and your own body-based, sensual reactions to the world around you.

CHAKRA THREE: THINKER

You are the thinker of the energy system. You revel in ideas, facts, information, and concepts and are driven to organize this information into understandable systems. Because of this, you are a great organizer and administrator. You have the ability to set up the structures necessary to meet your own or others' goals. Your spiritual destiny will, without a doubt, include working mindfully with knowledge to structure information-processes.

Chakra Color: Your color is YELLOW.

Third Auric Field: The third auric field attracts information that will be helpful to your goals, then organizes this information so your body and brain can interpret it. When finished with data gathering, this field then emits information back to the world, which is why so many people perceive you as bright and intelligent.

Chakra Development: This chakra is developed between ages 2½ and 4½, during which time you personalize others' reactions to your ideas, beliefs, and expression of personal power. Because of this, the third chakra houses issues about personal power, self-esteem, self-confidence, beliefs, and worldly success.

Chakra Four: Relater

Is there a relationship in the house? You'll gravitate right to that couple and within minutes be able to tell them what's working and what's not in their relationship. Because of your relationship-sensitivity, love and happiness are important to you, as is the tendency to want to heal or fix others' relationship problems. This focus can potentially thrust you into the world of healing, the act of serving others selflessly. No matter what, your spiritual purpose will involve helping others relationally or through healing endeavors.

Chakra Color: Your color is GREEN.

Fourth Auric Field: Your fourth auric field interprets others' relationship desires and needs and is actively engaged in helping you meet your own relationship needs. It can also send and receive healing energy, the energy and information necessary to help when others are ill, sad, anxious, or needy.

Chakra Development: This chakra opens between ages 4½ and 6½, and holds your personal ideas about love and relationships. Therefore, you will be strongly affected by issues relating to love, companionship, heart's desires, and health.

Chakra Five: Communicator

If you can't say it, you'll find a different way to communicate what you're thinking. Music, reading, speaking—anything goes as long as you get the message across. You are the verbal communicator of the chakra system, the person who best idealizes being opinionated and expressive, listening and understanding, and learning by hearing. Your spiritual destiny will inevitably involve communication, either through the so called normal channels of talking, speaking, or being musical or through conveying the mystical or spiritual messages that are passed to and through you.

Chakra Color: Your color is BLUE.

Fifth Auric Field: The fifth auric field conveys information-energy from practical and supernatural sources. You can potentially connect with spiritual guides, musical sources, and individuals' minds through this field.

Chakra Development: The fifth chakra develops between ages 6½ and 8½, calling forth the need to verbally communicate needs, desires, and opinions. Your primary life learning will involve setting boundaries, being responsible, and voicing concerns for self and others.

Chakra Six: Visionary

When it comes to long-term, you're already there! Why look to the past when the future beckons? If you're gifted in the sixth chakra, you're a long-range strategist, a big-picture thinker and are future-oriented. You'll also process information visually, transforming thoughts or senses into pictures. Your spiritual purpose will call on your ability to see into and help create a desirable future for yourself and for others.

Chakra Color: Your color is PURPLE.

Sixth Auric Field: The sixth auric field links you with potential futures and destiny paths. Upon choosing a path, this chakra then projects it forward so you and others can journey into and make decisions about the future.

Chakra Development: The sixth chakra matures from age 8½ to 13. During these years, you internalize society's views of you, your gender, and others in your ethnic and socioeconomic group. Your major issues to transcend will involve self-image, body image, cultural imaginings, and ego.

CHAKRA SEVEN: SPIRITUALIST

In Biblical times, seventh chakra spiritualists were stoned for their gifts. As it is, life might now treat you a little more fairly, for you represent spiritual ideas, ideals, and thoughts to those around you. You'll gravitate toward sacred ideas and values, intrinsically understanding the differences between good, bad, and evil. Your sensitivities can be directed practically, such as in helping others determine their personal spiritual callings, or more esoterically, such as leading others in spiritual pursuits (as in ministry or spiritual direction). In the practical realm, you're able to sense truth and correct action. In the metaphysical world, you're able to perceive spirits and the spiritual realm. These traits cause you to be spiritually accurate and committed to a solid value system.

Chakra Color: Your color is WHITE.

Seventh Auric Field: The seventh auric field links you to the spiritual dimensions, attracting and repelling spiritual energies and beings.

Chakra Development: Activated between ages 13 and 21, the seventh chakra allows healing from life's injuries to date and encourages life choices that match your spiritual purpose.

Chakra Eight: Shaman

When the world moves to the right, the shaman turns to the left.

Shamans mediate between the worlds of nature, humanity, and spirits. Because of this shamans often perceive opportunities where others see dread, black in what others know as white, and goodness in what others might call bad. Able to "walk between these worlds," the shaman is highly mystical and often fascinated with what is often called magic or sorcery. The truth is, the shaman understands the interconnection between all and can command the power necessary to merge parts into a whole design. The shaman's spiritual purpose can take him or her into just about any profession, but it always involves learning about power, healing, and mysticism. Often called a heyoke or the trickster, the shaman operates like a bolt of lightning—striking you when and where you least expect. Sometimes the heyoke or contrarian uses humor when someone is sad, sometimes anger to make someone happy. Always they have a sense of their own power and what would empower others.

Chakra Color: Your color is BLACK or SILVER.

The Eighth Auric Field: The eighth auric field looks like a thin silver mesh that links all time periods into one center. It's similar to a room that opens to hundreds of hallways, each path leading to a different time period, place, or dimension. Individuals gifted as Shamans are the "time keepers" of the universe, able to see or visit the past, present, or potential futures.

Chakra Development: The eighth chakra opens between ages 21 and 28, ushering in issues and energies from the past to be incorporated into today.

Chakra Nine: Idealist

If there's a cause, you'll know about it; an ideal, you'll have analyzed and assessed it. You are life's idealist, able to perceive the grander concepts directing the universe and, hopefully, humanity's heart. The root cause of your idealism lies in your ability to perceive the soul of humanity within individuals. You know that everyone is here for a purpose, as do seventh chakra spiritualists. But you also understand that individuals are linked for higher causes, thus everything that occurs in life fits a greater pattern. In touch with this perspective, you are able to see patterns in what you and others do. Hence, your spiritual purpose will inevitably evolve to include creation of unity or harmony for a specific, sometimes global cause.

Chakra Color: Your color is GOLD.

Ninth Auric Field: The ninth auric field links with beings and entities called the Forms, Masters, and archetypal figures, all of which hold universal ideals and concepts to help humanity progress. This field staples these higher forces to an individual's soul, creating patterns and processes between the personal and the heavenly so you can call on higher help anytime you need.

Chakra Development: The ninth chakra expands between ages 28 and 35, calling individuals to their soul's purpose and higher helpers. It is also present during preconception to help your soul select the physical genetics necessary to achieve its destiny.

CHAKRA TEN: NATURALIST

You'll know naturalists by their homes, which you could also call their havens. The refrigerator will be stocked with organic rice and sprouts, the garden full of growing vegetables, the bedroom with futons and pure cotton garments, and the woodwork will be made of real wood. The naturalist is the most environmentally sensitive of all the chakric types, able to sense and feel what's occurring in nature. If there's an injured animal, you'll know it; a cut tree, you'll feel it. This sensitivity allows a link with everything of the earth and everyone who has walked the earth. In some individuals this creates a connection between themselves and their ancestors or between the self and indigenous cultures. Naturalists can fulfill just about any job in any industry, as they are dependable and practical, but are best suited for spiritual callings involving nature, home, real estate, death, dying, and the earth.

Chakra Color: Your color is BROWN.

Tenth Auric Field: The tenth auric field surrounds the body and relates the physical self to the earth, the natural kingdom, and the ancestors. It nurtures the body with natural elements while mirroring the body's physical conditions, often lifting disease or problems from the body for disposal into the natural environment.

Chakra Development: Engaged before birth, the tenth auric field holds the genetics selected for life. It then matures between ages 35 and 42, causing individuals to ground their spiritual calling into the real world.

CHAKRA ELEVEN: COMMANDER

The Commander is infatuated with the natural and spiritual forces composing the universe and creating change. At will, a trained Commander is able to summon these forces and bend them to his or her intention, much as Jesus used natural energies to walk on water and Uri Geller moved molecules to bend spoons. Your innate powers will build until you desire to impact the world with them. Signs along the way include a fascination with miracles, mystical phenomenon, spiritual and natural forces, laws and elements, and means for manipulating or persuading. Your gift is strong and your personality will be, too, as you are able to convert negative energies into neutral or positive forces, and vice versa. As you develop your gift, you'll naturally rise in any profession, although many Commanders prefer to strike out on their own, researching the information that supports their inner knowing.

Chakra Color: Your color is ROSE.

Eleventh Auric Field: The eleventh auric field links with natural and spiritual energy sources and elements and allows control of these forces through the entire auric field, but specifically through movement of the hands and feet.

Chakra Development: The eleventh chakra is strongest between ages 42 and 49, thereby allowing a natural Commander the time needed to develop a strong set of ethics and guidelines for instrumenting change. Many Commanders finally "make it" at this midlife point, having spent years learning and struggling before coming into their own.

UNDERSTANDING YOUR BASIC NATURE: YOUR CHAKRA PERSONALITY SCORE

Look up your quiz scores and compare them with the eleven basic chakra types. You're now going to assess your innate nature and from that get an idea as to your spiritual calling.

Fill in this box to get your line-up.

Chakra Personality Table

Place	Score	Title/s

Here's an example using my own scores.

Chakra Personality Table

Place	Score	Title/s
First place	30 points	1. Manifester 6. Visionary 8. Shaman
Second place	25 points	11. Commander
Third place	24 points	2. Feeler 5. Communicator 10. Naturalist
Fourth place	21 points	4. Relater
Fifth place	18 points	3. Thinker 7. Spiritualist
Sixth place	9 points	9. Idealist

You now have a picture of your gift order, strongest to weakest. Before putting together a full portrait of yourself or someone else, here is a tip. Label your chakras and gifts with these three titles:

Strong
Supportive
Weak

Strong chakras are those that are most developed and apt to contain your spiritual coding, gifts, and financial style. These are the chakras with the highest scores. Your supportive chakras fall in the middle range and are solid and functional. They can either complement your strong characteristics or take over when necessary. Your weak chakras represent your vulnerable or in-active areas. Usually, these chakras are weak because they aren't necessary to your spiritual unfolding. Sometimes the weakness is caused by damage or injury, usually from childhood experiences. In these cases, it is best to strengthen the weak chakra(s) through healing endeavors.

In general, the most important scores are your top three gifts and your lowest ones. These will tell you what you're really good at and really bad at. However, you can flesh out your self-portrait with the supportive chakras. As you create your own imaging, these pointers might help.

1. If you have one strong chakra.

You are very gifted in a certain area and it will probably be rela-tively simple to select a profession or an outlet for your spiritual nature. Other individuals will be easily able to see and respect your gift and support you in following it. Be careful to not get too "single-minded." Developing some of your other higher scoring abilities will add balance and stability.

2. If you have two strong chakras.

You are equally gifted in two areas, which can assure balance in your life. When one gift is questionable, you can rely on the other. You might also feel forced to choose between two very different sets of ideas, goals, or professions. Support both your gifts until you find a job or focus that unifies them and you will eventually become more successful and happier.

3. If you have three strong chakras.

You will be challenged to select a profession that enables you to use multiple strengths, but once you do, you will be able to move forward quickly. Picture the three chakra points as a triangle. You might need to pick one quality or gift for the topside of the tri-angle to serve as your lead service or business, with the other two providing support and backbone. Know that you can change these around. Some three-chakra people run three businesses at a time; others work in a single area but provide multiple services. For instance, someone with the Relater might put this first to be a homemaker, but use his or her Communicator gift to serve on PTAs and a Thinking gift to attend school part-time. Later, the Thinking gift can take over as an entrée into the workplace.

4. If you have four strong chakras.
You might feel pulled in many directions! If you have four strong gifts, you must get organized. It might well be worth using a career counselor for assistance if you need it. The easiest way to examine your abilities energetically is to view your gifts as four corners in a square or a rectangle. Each gift supports the other in a stable environment. Now ask, what types of environments will help you multitask in a secure way? You'll want to select a profession that enables expression of all gifts simultaneously, but this may take a long time.

5. If you have more than four strong chakras.
Multiple chakra strengths can be confusing. Typically, individuals in this category feel overwhelmed, overburdened, and lack psychic and social boundaries, which can lead to problems including depression and anxiety. It's like being given so many birthday gifts that you can't decide which to open first! Work with a therapist and a trained intuitive to establish good psychological, emotional, physical, and psychic boundaries, and then pick a chakra and go for it. Use your other talents as secondary and supportive gifts. Ironically, individuals with multiple talents like yours generally prosper by developing their weakest chakras as well. These chakras can often balance the strongest and lead to more peace of mind.

6. If your chakras are mainly in the midrange.
You are probably an easy-going and likeable person, but sometimes feel like you have no true abilities or gifts. The truth is, you

probably do have a strong chakra but are either unable to test for it or, for various reasons, are hiding it deep inside. Sometimes, our childhood family squelches our natural expression, usually out of fear or judgment. If you think this is the case, return to your childhood memories. What did you like to do? What were your early gifts and desires? What attributes and goals were important to you when you were young? By approaching your gifts "backward to forward," you'll uncover your true nature and be able to develop it energetically.

7. If you have a lot of weak chakras.

Some individuals have a lot of weaker chakras. Frankly, there's nothing wrong with this, as long as you also have at least one strong chakra. Our world tends to applaud gifts and mock weaknesses. The truth is, we can't be all things to all people, nor should we try. Knowing your weaknesses is key to compensating for them. Surround yourself with people who have your missing gifts and enjoy being humble. If you have a lot of weak chakras and all your other chakras are in the middle range, however, you are probably under the cloud of low self-esteem and aren't realistically assessing your abilities. You might want to work with a professional to unearth the reasons for your low self-worth.

DRAWING DOWN THE STARS:
DOING A CHAKRA CONSTELLATION ASSESSMENT

It's time to put together your own chakra constellation or picture of your chakra gifts. Here are a few questions that will get you started on your own constellation. You can also use this process to examine someone else's chakra personality.

Fill in these questions for yourself or someone else to create a chakra assessment.

I am reviewing: _____ (your name or someone else, if doing this for another person.)

These are his or her strongest chakras and corresponding character traits:

The total of these strongest chakra traits means that s/he is interested in the following:

And that s/he will usually act like this:

And that s/he will want the following out of life:

And that s/he will help others these ways:

Based on _____'s strengths, I would suggest that his or her spiritual purpose involves the following:

These are _____'s supportive chakras and corresponding character traits:

The total of these supportive chakra traits means that s/he is interested in the following:

And that s/he will act like this under pressure:

And that s/he can do the following to compensate for strong weaknesses:

And that s/he can do the following to support meeting his or her spiritual purpose:

These are _____'s weak chakras and corresponding character deficiencies:

The total of these weak chakras means that s/he will lack the ability or drive to:

And that s/he will not be interested in:

And that s/he will be vulnerable to:

And that s/he might need to do the following to compensate:

In three sentences, I would now describe _____ like this:

Some people feel funny analyzing themselves. It's not as hard as it seems. The truth is, assessing your chakras is an objective process. I encourage people to take their own scores and assessment and write them in paragraph form. This gives you a complete overview of yourself and develops a base for determining your money style, which we will do next.

As an example, I'm going to analyze myself using my own scores and answers to the chakra constellation assessment. I have not included my specific answers here, just the write-up.

Given her scores, even a stranger would now be able to get a pretty clear picture of Cyndi Dale. Let's analyze her as if she were a stranger, shall we?

Cyndi's strong gifts are extremely strong, emphasizing physicality, vision, and mysticism. Her chakra scores indicate she is interested in the everyday world and attracted to material objects and success. A long-term planner, she is able to bring her strategic and visual abilities into play and set goals for obtaining material success, but can also employ the mystical visional gifts to peer between the various planes of existence available to the Shaman. I would say that this woman's mission involves manifesting mystical realities in the physical plane to bring long-term change on earth.

Cyndi has a lot of supportive chakras. Scoring in at 24 and 25, her first tier of supportive chakras lend her skills at commanding, feeling, communicating, and understanding the natural and historical. These supportive chakras are fairly balanced among themselves, a nice mix of soft and hard, love and power based—unlike her top chakra configuration. Her strong chakras mark her as an overachiever who is driven to gain power to meet her goals. She could easily burn out or lose perspective about the artistic or softer aspects of life. Her first-tier support system still upholds her push for power through the Commander influence, but also encourages feeling, creating, and restoration. I would suggest that she stays connected to people she loves and considers taking on a creative hobby, especially if it can involve her home or land, such as decorating or gardening. Her Naturalist tendencies can therefore help her replenish and renew.

The difference between the first-tier support level and the next, with a jump to 21 then to 18, is fairly nominal. And so, I would also see Cyndi's relational gift as an important adjunct to her larger mission. This second-tier supportive chakra can help Cyndi when under stress, fill out information her highest intuitive abilities might miss, and add balance to her life. The Spiritualist and Thinking attributes are balanced. These gifts enable her to care about others yet remain separate from their problems.

Cyndi's relative weaknesses in the spiritual and soul chakras point to potential difficulties holding onto God's larger picture or universal ethics. A quick read of Cyndi's chart would emphasize a lack of idealism. This obvious limitation could mean that she could "cut corners" in achieving her goals and could become too aggressive, to the point of hurting others. She should develop a clear set of ethics that are not materialist and stick to them, in order to contain her powers and abilities. At the same time, I would suggest that lacking the idealism means that causes won't interfere with her drive to success.

Based on her constellation, I'd also encourage Cyndi to constantly work on boundaries, emotional or universal, as she can potentially engage power for destructive as well as constructive ends depending upon how she feels. As well, she would be wise to hire others to assist her with structure, whether in her household or business. Though she has the ability with a supportive third chakra, the mystical will occupy more of her interest and therefore, her basic life organization could deflate.

Do you see how a basic chakra read can set the stage for figuring out your spiritual purpose and gifts and life plan? There's nothing to be embarrassed about, remember that! We have strengths and weaknesses for a reason, the reason-maker being the Divine. Your scoring constellation might not be anything like mine. It probably won't be. But you can still figure out what your chakra constellation is telling you about yourself.

From Purpose to Prosperity:
Your Money Style

Says Tanaquil: "But what are they,
the Inner Worlds? Dreams?"

Answers Jaive: "Not at all. Places that might be.
Places where we can meet with ourselves."

*"But it was **real**."*

"Perhaps," said Jaive softly,
*"now you've **made** it real."*[6]

The Invitation to Abundance

Our chakras reveal the inner worlds of the universe, the very portals that invite Spirit and spiritual forces to dance. By opening these doors, we can welcome the energies needed to create abundance.

Abundance first exists in the dream world, where we first image or imagine our needs and desires. Our goals and hopes are more than fantasy, however, when they are anchored in our energy system. Our spirit expresses our inner self through our energy centers, which marries our purpose to our everyday life. Life itself welcomes abundance.

We all want the stars to come to earth. Your spirit has already issued the invitation and is ready to accept the prosperity and money needed to fulfill your destiny. Quite simply, you are programmed to make enough money to assure the accomplishment of your spiritual destiny. By tracking your goals, attitudes, behavior, and intuition through your chakra system, you assure yourself the monetary support you need to live an exciting and fulfilling life. By working with your finances inside of the boundaries of your chakra types and gift orders, you can actually push through the boundaries that have limited you thus far.

Your Money Personality

Each chakra and personality type envisions money in a different way. And each chakra type will attract, manage, save, and spend money uniquely. A Feeler, for instance, would never think of money as a driving force. Compassionate by nature and investing in generating, money is a means to an end. A Feeler would never "sell out." To a Feeler, you don't exchange creativity or happiness for mere money. A Manifester, on the other hand, can easily equate money with happiness. Money is a means to an end because with money, you can create more tangible resources. A Manifester would have no compunction pulling off a deal simply to gain more money.

Is a Feeler foolish? A Manifester manipulative? Feelers can be foolish and Manifesters, maneuvering but not because of innate goals, desires, and monetary tendencies. Feelers create because they must. It's coded into their destiny. Manifesters manifest because they are spiritually compelled to do so. They build the buildings that Feelers and Visionaries design.

Your innate worldview of money will affect how you approach financial decision making. If you inherently put causes before money, as does an Idealist, you might reject most moneymaking ventures in favor of goodwill. By reframing the perspective of self, however, an Idealist can begin to understand that money can support a cause and can therefore be important for achieving a higher spiritual purpose.

By assessing your inner nature, you can begin to better understand and illustrate your money personality, your particular way of making and managing money for abundance. Let's look at each of the eleven major personality types from the financial point of view, so you can become familiar with your prosperity consciousness. I'll highlight the following in terms of each chakra type in relation to moneymaking and management:

- Style
- Needs
- Values
- Drives
- Strengths
- Weaknesses
- Success tips (including potential career options)
- Dealing with debt and financial problems
- Methods for decision-making

CHAKRA ONE MONEY STYLE: MANIFESTER

Style: As a physical person, your perception of money is material. Money is a real and tangible resource to you, something you can understand because it creates material success. You like money and buying goods with it, the higher the quality the better.

Because of your materialistic orientation, you will approach moneymaking as a goal unto itself. You'll feel good every time you make another buck and, likewise, save another dollar. As a Manifester, you approach money as you do everything else: physically. You'll work daily toward financial affluence just as you exercise daily. You'll study and read about financial concepts, assess investments for optimum returns, and in general, consider making money to be as vital as watching your health.

Needs: You will need money the same way that you require air, food, water, housing, clothing, and touch to survive. Of all the chakra types, Manifesters understand that money makes the world go around. Because you comprehend the basic sense of having money, you will desire to see your money increase over time. Because you are so physical, your financial success will affect your physical health. The healthier your pocketbook, the healthier your body. The more solid your investments, the more secure you will feel.

Values: Making money is a value of yours, as is increasing personal wealth. This creed is basic to your value system and you will strive to use money to provide for others' primary needs as well as your own. In regard to family and loved ones, your ethic includes making sure that their basic needs are met and that they, too, understand the need to be financially stable and responsible. Monetary responsibility will measure high on your assessment of self and others, and you will tend to trust people who are more rather than less capable of managing their money. While you don't require things or material possessions in and of themselves, you do consider the ability to purchase and provide a measure of respectability and accountability.

Drives: Manifesters are driven to make more and more money, usually through endeavors that create tangible, practical, and solid products. Certainly, you are service-oriented, but in general, if you can make money for yourself or someone else, that's considered the best service of all!

Strengths: Of all the chakra types, yours is the best at understanding and making money. You're not afraid of money and are able to create material safety and security for yourself and others. You are a good provider and thrive on providing for others' and your own basic needs.

Weaknesses: Not everything in life can be weighed against financial success. Driven to succeed financially, you can pass up opportunities for relationships, rest and relaxation, and spiritual pursuits. It's too easy for you to become slave to the "Almighty Dollar." You must strive for interests besides business or money by looking at the real purchasing value of the dollar: time for love and enjoyment.

Success tips: Because you perceive success in tangible, measurable terms, your easiest ways to make money is through physical and active endeavors. Here are some specific pointers for making money:

- Create, sell, or service products that are tangible and practical.
- Market your physical prowess. Manifesters make the best owners and active professionals in areas of health and wellness, exercise and gyms, and all sports.
- Work directly with or in money. Finance, stock investing, venture capital, banking, and insurance are all money-driven businesses. You're a natural at energizing enterprises to make money.
- As the most natural entrepreneur of the chakra system, you're good at starting—and not as good at running—businesses or business operations. Get someone else to do the day-to-day and follow-through tasks, and keep yourself focused on your goals.

- Invest in your own business or others businesses that are hard-core and serve primary needs. You'll understand anything that has to do with housing, real estate, and land; clothing or retail; food, food service, or food distribution; air or air quality; fuel or fuel products; transportation; and basic health and welfare.
- Keep your eye on quality not quantity. Your best returns are from investing in quality driven operations, businesses, stocks, art, or collectibles.
- Don't evaluate your own self-worth on your bottom-line or cash flow. You'll be tempted to do so.
- Consider teaching or mentoring once you've become well-established. Your ethic calls for you to share your hard-earned knowledge with others and to enable their success.

Dealing with debt and financial problems: Debt and downside turns will affect you, perhaps more than any other chakra type. You sense prosperity issues in your body, and your body will mirror what's going on for you financially. You can get through crises by doing the following:

- Make sure you take care of your physical health. When the dollar plunges below the waistline, watch your own waistline. Monitor your diet, sleeping, and exercise regime for optimum health.
- Look to your past. You've already achieved some modicum of success or you wouldn't be depressed when the going gets tough. Manifesters often experience ups and downs because they're willing to take chances. Remember that every downswing in your wake was followed by an upswing, or you wouldn't have reached the pinnacle you've just fallen from!
- Pay off debt. Put your first earnings toward debt repayment. Manifesters feel all financial burdens in their physi-

cal bodies. Debt will affect your health. Get out of debt and you'll be better able to make more money. If you need to do so, sell resources to get solvent. You'll feel lighter and more clear headed.

- Count your blessings during a down time. If you can't count your financial resources right now, appreciate your other blessings. Downturns are a good time to assess the real meaning of life—and your relationships.
- Watch the market. You'll have an innate physical sense of what consumers will buy or not and how certain markets might turn or not.
- If you don't think you're manifesting to your capabilities, work through any issues relating to safety and security, worth and deserving. Manifesters' issues often pertain to preverbal experiences. If money is a continual challenge, look into your early childhood. If money or work has become addictive, you absolutely must probe your childhood for reasons you might be substituting something you "can't take with you" for love and happiness. Addictions often strike manifesters, as the source of many hard-core addictions lies within the first chakra and in early life experiences.

Methods for decision making: You can use your physical sensitivity to gain financial advantage. As a Manifester, you are intuitively gifted with what I call physical sympathy, the ability to sense external conditions in your own body. For instance, Manifesters are able to hold an object and sense the owner's personality. Your body can mirror others' physical illnesses or circumstances. You may think you have a cold because someone else does. You might suddenly feel poor when a friend loses money in the market.

You can also intuit an investment potential in your own body. If you are considering a certain stock, purchase, or financial opportunity, for instance, your body will respond to a good investment with an upbeat physical sensation. If the opportunity isn't fruitful, you'll most likely feel tired or down. Believe your body for moneymaking and management decisions.

Stick to what you know. If you're most comfortable with money ideas or management opportunities that cover primal needs, look there for your investment ideas. Buy real estate or houses, invest in stocks producing tangible goods, look at inventions that meet primary concerns or body needs, and make your money by investing in your ultimately most intelligent investment—yourself!

Want a role model? Consider Michael Jordan of basketball fame; Andrew Carnegie, who invented the steel industry; Henry Ford, who engineered the car industry and invented the assembly line; Mary Kay of Mary Kay Cosmetics, who created an entire in-home beauty industry; and Ben and Jerry of Ben and Jerry's Ice Cream, who took a food item and revolutionized it.

CHAKRA TWO MONEY STYLE: FEELER

Style: You are the most feeling based of the chakric types. You perceive yourself, others, situations, and money through the lens of emotions. In regard to money, if you're happy, you'll be more successful financially. If you're unhappy, you'll be less successful financially.

One of your most profitable emotional expressions is through your creativity. Sensual in nature, you will be drawn toward the creative, even in terms of money. While others might consider you financially carefree, the truth is, you want money only if it will spark or further your artistic drive. Along these lines, you'll prosper most if you're creative in how you make, save, and perceive money.

Needs: Feelers don't actually perceive money as a true need. In fact, you'll probably consider money as nothing more than a necessary or possibly unnecessary evil. To you, money might get in the way of creative actions, although you do need money to buy the basics for creative endeavors. Money can seemingly inhibit the rich world of emotions. Consider how many individuals feel bad because they don't have money! You'll be more open to manifesting money if you stop trying to "need" money. Instead, desire what money can create or how it can assist.

Values: Money isn't a core value. Your main joys involve feeling good, being sensual, helping others to feel good, and being creative.

Drives: You are driven to work through your feelings and to better understand others' feelings. You are also driven to succeed at being creative or in changing ugliness to beauty. You can use these drives to make money or to justify the need to have money.

Strengths: Your financial strengths include being able to understand how others feel under differing financial conditions. You will have compassion for the poor or indebted and feel happy for those whose monetary success is expanding.

Weaknesses: Because you can easily perceive money as a source for negative feelings, you might sabotage your efforts at moneymaking. The creative urge tends to be chaotic. You might have difficulties organizing your money, the business side of a creative venture, budgeting, or following a savings and investment program.

Success tips: Use your feelings and your creativity! The following might help:

- Invest in your own creative endeavors. Start the unusual, not the obvious.
- You will feel most successful if your money comes through feeling-based work, such as counseling or helping others, or through creative and artistic endeavors that are expressive in nature.
- You are also very creative and can see financial opportunities where others cannot. Use this gift to scope out un-

common investments or products or to invent new or re-packaged services.

- If you lack an organizational chakra, partner with a more businesslike person or hire administrative help. Let someone else keep the books.
- Follow your feelings. If a certain market product or service seems to make people feel good, evaluate it for an investment opportunity.
- Only take jobs that make you feel happy. Otherwise, you'll get too depressed and you'll fail.
- Watch your carbohydrate consumption. If you're overdoing the yeast and bread products, you might be absorbing others' feelings or hiding the unhappiness in your life.
- Stay away from negative people or negative-sounding investments. You easily absorb other's feelings and this will adversely affect your reasoning ability.
- Connect your creativity with others' bottom-line needs. Are you an artist? Everyone needs his or her walls painted: Become a wall artist!
- Don't confuse compassion with being foolish. Just because someone is in a sad or bad place, you don't need to support him or her financially. Be careful. Don't caretake.
- Save your money creatively. Paint your piggy bank. Get colored savings account checkbooks. Put a poster on the wall and give yourself a star whenever you put money in a mutual fund. Have fun and the world will smile back!

Dealing with debt and financial problems: Here are some ideas for the Feeler who needs to feel his or her way out of a bad situation.

- If you are having true money difficulties, get a financial planner. If your problem is that you lack one of the administrative chakras, a professional can really be supportive. If you have some sort of structural gift in your chakra system, consider asking wise and thoughtful friends for help—especially those with good money sense. Hold a brainstorming session. Ask your friends to come up with creative moneymaking solutions for you. They might be able to help you turn an innate gift of compassion or a creative and artistic expression into a moneymaking opportunity.

- If you're really down in the dumps, get a therapist. Figure out which inhibiting feelings are yours and which belong to other individuals. Feelers pick up others' feelings. Sometimes lack of success can be due to depressive feelings actually belonging to someone else!

- Know, too, that anything that blocks your feelings or your creativity will inhibit financial success. Consider getting professional help to work through any issues imparted from ages 6 months to 2½ years, the years in which your second chakra opened. These years are feeling in nature and involve exploring how others deal with our creative expression. If at any point you sublimated beliefs that you must inhibit yourself to be loved, your money flow will be limited. Taking care of yourself first and others second is a good start to healing success blocks. Using your innate gifts of compassion and mercy will help you heal and leave you ready for success.

Methods for decision making: Want to figure out a good investment of time or money? Here are some processes to entertain.

- See how the opportunity makes you feel. Actually monitor your feelings for a day, concentrating on your question. If an idea makes you happy, it might work. Sad, it won't.

- Considering a purchase? Hold an art object. Do you feel joy at holding it? This sensation could indicate that the product will hold or increase in value over time. Always choose what is beautiful or sacred to you and you'll appreciate your own decisions, if not make money.

- Talk with friends or write in a journal until you know your true emotional reactions to a situation or opportunity.
- Never, never, never make a choice until you've seen all the options. You're creative! If you see only one choice, create another option. Two choices? Create a third. Then choose.

You're in good company as a Feeler! Famous Feelers include Vincent Van Gogh, the painter; Georgia O'Keefe, the painter; Benjamin Franklin, who continually created new inventions and political viewpoints; Dr. Joyce Brothers, a professional sex adviser and author; and Dear Abby, whose advice columns splashed everyone awake.

CHAKRA THREE MONEY STYLE: THINKER

Style: You are an information junkie. Give you information, you can set about the task of organizing, cataloguing, and compartmentalizing, lining up your facts or sums in neat and orderly columns. When it comes to money, you want to know where your money is, where it came from, where it's going, and what to do to get more money. Whether or not you are actually an accountant, you'll be able to give an accounting for every penny earned and spent.

Needs: Money is important to you, but well-managed money is even more important. Your true financial need isn't really having money. It's being successful. Success will be determined by how much personal power you exercise in the workplace, or in your home if you're a homemaker. You need to feel empowered for your efforts and rewarded by being noticed. Money is simply a means of evaluating success and assuring recognition.

Values: You value that which builds the mind. This can include education, learning, and thinking processes. Order is important to you because it prevents fear. You don't like to feel like information can be used against you or to hurt someone else. Because of this, you value structure, organization, and common sense.

Drives: A third chakra person is typically driven to succeed, but not for financial purposes alone. You want to achieve goals by following a logical path that builds your own and others' self-esteem. While you can easily achieve positional power, as in a high title, it's even more important to wield personal power, to be recognized for being vital. Making money is great, but you'll be even more driven to organize your money logically.

Strengths: You're great at budgeting. Even better, you can actually stay within a budget because your mind can account for every penny in your pocket! When it comes to surveying investments, you're a solid technical analyst. Whether the investment is in purchasing clothing for your son's Little League or buying a stock, you'll run a comparison-analysis and cost-benefit ratio that will make the more creative chakra types weak kneed. Because you're so good with managing money, you're a natural at helping others with their money. As long as they listen to you, that is.

Weaknesses: Managing money can seem a logical function, but it's not. Consumers and investors are fickle, as are our children and spousal units! You might think you've built a plan and it's going to stay put, but people change the equation. Hence, you can experience frustration unless you allow for fluidity and creativity.

Your analytic abilities can easily result in you becoming too controlling. You can become too scared if money doesn't flow according to your expectations and therefore too controlling of yourself or others.

Success tips: Your research and intuitive faculties can serve you equally well in determining a wise versus unwise investment opportunity. You'll need to read the balance sheets, of course, along with all the other applicable and structural information. "Analyze,

analyze, analyze," might as well be your motto. In line with your natural style, you can also do the following:

- Lend your abilities to the less organized—and charge them for your input!
- Set a budget and follow it, but build in a margin for error or for human change.
- Disconnect your self-esteem from workplace or home place success. You simply can't control everyone else. Instead, link your esteem to your value system and your learning process.
- Consider investing in an education. You're bright. Schools tend to reward quick thinkers like you.
- Be self-confident. Self-esteem measures our internal opinions of ourselves; self-confidence expresses how we think others see us. Assume that others find your assistance, information, organizational abilities, and structural skills helpful. They will.
- Assess others' goals to see if you can clearly throw yourself behind them. You'll feel better at the end of the day if you can buy into others' plans, as well as your own.
- Be patient with those less organized than you. They may not have the same skills.
- Consider having different bank accounts to separate your various life needs. This can help you stay organized financially.
- Become an expert. You can easily "niche market" and become a valued employee, consultant, or volunteer.
- Watch your consumption of caffeine, coca-colas, or beer. Caffeine often creeps up when Thinkers don't like their jobs or works; consequently, they turn to artificial stimulants to keep motivated. The same is true of your dark colas, though heavy cola use tends to indicate that a Thinker is in a situation costing his or her self-esteem. Beer can indicate that a Thinker is uncomfortable regarding self-confidence,

and might need to accept him or herself instead of relying
on external acceptance.

- Consider careers that rely upon information, structural
skills, and analytical abilities. You'll usually find a Thinker
leading an operational department, running an accounting business, teaching technical information, or serving
as an administrator, lawyer, stock broker, investment or
systems analyst, mortgage banker, homemaker, PTA president, or information specialist.

- If you don't feel as successful as you could be, consider
probing your past to deal with internalized resistance to
success. Many of your issues will be fear based and might
stem from the years between 2½ and 4½, when you were
learning how to interface with the world. These are the
power years. Depending upon how well your ideas and
concepts were received, you'll decide whether you deserve success or not. If you think you do, you'll have high
self-esteem and high self-confidence. Failure won't stop
you. You'll just try again, intelligently assessing why you
failed so you don't do it again. If your earlier expressions
weren't received or you were shamed, you'll be afflicted
with low self-esteem and low self-confidence. You won't
think you deserve success. You'll be too scared to assert
yourself in money or workplace concerns. Get in touch
with your natural energy and your organizational abilities and you can sail!

Dealing with debt and financial problems: Your tendency will be to
compartmentalize your debt or financial difficulties. Frankly, this
is smart. We can be "up" in one area and "down" in another. If you
have a hard time seeing the big picture, however, get help from a
consultant. You don't want to rob Peter to pay Paul if this puts
you in financial jeopardy or further debt. As you're uniquely able
to do of all the chakra types, create an accounting system for paying back debt or digging out of a hole. Run the numbers for figur-

ing out if you need to declare bankruptcy, take out a loan or contact your creditors to make your own payback arrangements.

Methods for decision making: You will tend toward making decisions using logic, facts, and reason. Remember that you are also highly intuitive in an area called mental sympathy. This means that through your third auric field, you can access psychic data that pertains to your questions or needs. By learning how to trust your "gut sense," you can give yourself a spiritual advantage, useful for those who are especially mental in nature. Always, however, use your intelligence when assessing investments or work opportunities. You can easily create a sheet with "plus" and "minus" columns to negotiate decision making.

Of all the chakra types, logic is most advantageous to you. Regarding investments, take a class on reading an annual report. Because you can so easily and quickly educate yourself, consider becoming an expert in a specific field or with a particular investment strategy.

Join the crowd of famous Thinkers by stretching backward in time. There are Madame Curie and Albert Einstein of science fame and Pythagoras of mathematics. More current Thinkers include Bill Gates of Microsoft and Dr. Candace Pert, who reflects a Feeler interest in emotion with hard-core research science. A Thinking-Healer is Barbara Ann Brennan, a NASA scientist who now teaches about energy medicine.

CHAKRA FOUR MONEY STYLE: RELATER

Style: You are a healer and life's relationship expert. If there's relationship that can be fixed, you'll ferret it out and band-aid it again and again! And everything in life is about relationship, isn't it? Including business and money.

When it comes to money, you will probably tend to be either highly thrifty or very spendy. Frugal Relaters have figured out that the best way to deal with their relationship sensitivities is to pull in and protect themselves. In line with this reasoning, they will hold money tight to their chests. Spendy Relaters might run money the way that they dole out gossip. A little here, a little there—and pretty soon there's no control! Bottom line, a Relater will handle money the same way that he or she handles relationships.

Needs: Money is less important than your heart's desires because you are a heart-based person. Your needs will reflect your heart's deepest needs and wishes. Money is therefore a means to an end. It's a way to obtain your heart's desires, and a way to make relationships run smoothly. If a loved one is shy of cash, you'll feel like you need money—not for yourself, but for your friend! Your needs follow your perception of relationships and can change as relationships change.

Values: You value love, relationship, and healing above all else. Because of this, money is a means to an end. You see what's broken and want to make it whole. Money is the great salve of humanity. If it can fix a broken heart, a ruined company, or a rejected stock, you'll use it for that purpose. Your money has to make a difference, thus you'll be more successful when you're making a difference with your money.

Drives: You are driven to succeed at relationships above any other concerns. Because of this, you'll put your money behind your relationships or even into healing yourself from relationships! This drive can motivate you to make money to help yourself and other people; take care of your children, spouse, or parents; or raise money to help others who have been injured in any way.

Strengths: Because you're so apt at reading relationships, you're the perfect candidate to assess certain aspects of investment opportunities. You can easily perform assessments of corporate management teams, employee strengths and weaknesses, health-care institutions and their effectiveness, and any other relationship-based information sources.

Weaknesses: You can give yourself away without meaning to do so. As a Relater, it's all too easy to put others' needs before your own, or to hold back your own success so you don't hurt or challenge someone else. You might pull out of a successful deal because it threatens your spouse or give up a good job because it would tip the balance at home. Your drive to help others heal is exhausting and can take all your energy.

Success tips: Use your relationship strengths to review jobs, investment opportunities, and career-related situations. You'll know who is honest or not, or what systems support people or not. Make sure, however, you constantly watch your boundaries. Put yourself first. Put others second, unless there's a real need to do otherwise. Other tips include:

- Understand the issue of "energy exchange." If you're going to give energy to someone else, you need energy back. The return can be in the guise of monetary payment, time, or even appreciation, but it needs to be there for you to prosper.
- Consider careers that are relationship based. You can realize abundance in arenas including healing and health care, medicine, counseling, negotiation, employee management, nonprofit management or service, personnel and human relations, animal care, and other heart-based endeavors.
- Do you feel like someone stands at the door of your heart, preventing success? Your main success blocks were probably incurred from ages 4½ to 6½, the relationship years of life, or in later relationships. How did others deal with your heart? How did the adults around you manage love? Were they loving or not? If you were provided enough love,

you'll feel comfortable attracting enough money. If love was restricted, your finances will be restricted. Deal with issues like "I don't deserve" or "I'm not loveable" in order to attract your heart's desires and, therefore, your financial returns.

• Watch your sugar and wine intake. Heart-based people feel deeply and often feel others' needs even more deeply than they feel their own. If you're big into sugar or wine, you're probably losing yourself in a relationship. You won't move forward personally if you're carrying someone else.

• You'll prosper with investments of time and money if concerns are healing driven. Health care, hospitals, and therapeutic clinics will be top on the list, but so are investments that assist the needy or less fortunate. This can include products that are medical or even financial in nature—as long as they help not hurt people or animals.

• By examining the relationship between a selected investment, business, or service and all the stakeholders or individuals affected, you can decide what's worth your while or not. Want to make a good investment? Figure out who's being healed. If someone or something is being improved, you can put your heart—and pocketbook—behind it.

Dealing with debt and financial problems: Here are a few ideas.

• First, determine if debt-related problems are your own or another person's doing. Many fourth chakra individuals carry others' financial burdens out of care and misunderstanding. If you're doing this, seek the appropriate help to sort yourself out. Consider a therapist if it's difficult to think of securing your own needs.

• Seek legal counsel if necessary to figure out how to sort your money from someone else's. Even in marriage, you deserve to be financially secure and protected from someone else's irresponsibility.

- If the financial straits are your own doing, seek financial counseling.

- As a Relater, consider getting a financial counselor no matter what. You're probably pretty busy gathering input from lots of sources. It's like pollinating: drop a little of your problem here and pick up a thought over there. Unless you're energetically backed by an organizationally oriented chakra, you probably aren't very good at putting all this advice together—or at budgeting, financial assessments, or the like. You'll be excellent at determining monetary needs, especially for your family, but not so good at writing a roadmap. Compensate by hiring the help you need.

- Don't confuse love with money. Stop giving away your money, if you're doing so!

- Get paid what you're worth. You might love your job, but you deserve to be paid. Remember the idea of "energy exchange?" Make sure you're compensated fairly or get a new job.

Methods for decision making: No matter the issue, you will sense reactions in your heart. You will automatically condense situations into relationship compartments and analyze relationships for their content. Make use of this. One of the easiest energy techniques is to imagine red energy from your first chakra moving upward through your body. Join it with white energy from your seventh chakra. Mix these two energies in your heart and create a pink bubble. Extend this bubble outside of your body. Next, ask a question. Step into the pink bubble and allow it to open to your answer. This exercise merges spiritual with physical energies to allow a loving response.

Another good fourth chakra exercise is to think of a choice

and picture yourself placing this option in your heart for a set amount of time, say an hour, overnight, or for a day. Then gauge your reaction to this choice. How did it feel? What sensations did it impose? You can do the same with yet another choice and weigh one alternative against another.

Relationship experts of the world—welcome YOU! Join Dr. Phil, who now has his own talk show on relationship problems in America; Oprah, who founded an entire talk show based on her relationship skills; Sigmund Freud, who started it all; Louise Hay, healer and author who saw the relationships between illness and feelings; and Amma, a Hindu Master who is known as the saint who has given a million hugs.

Chakra Five Money Style: Communicator

Style: You are the communicator of the chakra system. Because of this, when money is involved you'll probably read everything you can get your hands on, talk to anyone who'll respond, and listen to as many experts as possible. In the end, however, you have the best source of all as your investment counselor: the Divine. While you're busy taking and giving information, you've a lifeline of pure knowledge between your fifth chakra and the One Upstairs.

Needs: You need to communicate. This doesn't sound like an extremely complex need, but think about how many types of communication there are—and how few people are really good at saying what they think! Most people are raised to sublimate their real needs to others, to stray toward dishonesty in attempts to save others' feelings, and to put others' needs before their own. You need others to be straightforward and clear. You also need them to listen and respond to you. When speaking doesn't work, you'll resort to writing. And for some of you, writing or music is your best expression anyway! Know that you need to communicate to create yourself in the world, and you prize others who do the same. Against this backdrop, money is simply a means to an end. You don't need money itself; you need the communication vehicles and the time for communicating that money can purchase.

Values: Honesty, truth, and expression are your three major values. Because you innately understand what others are trying to communicate, you will perceive the differences between what they're saying and what they're really thinking. This is challenging. You'll react to salespeople who are lying, bosses who don't tell the truth, and loved ones who don't express what they really want or need. Of course, you apply your spiritual value system in the financial area, too.

Drives: You're more driven toward truthful self-expression than making money. You do want to be recognized and rewarded for your expressive abilities and will press forward until you achieve satisfaction. Whatever your communication style or outlet, it will push you until you let yourself out.

Strengths: Financially, your strengths lend themselves to analyzing communications to make monetary decisions. Your intuitive abilities include verbal sympathy, which means you hear guidance and information psychically. By developing this innate gift you'll process data with clarity and know what to say or reply in return. You can present anything from a product to an idea for training and sell just about anything with your incredible presentation skills.

Weaknesses: Unless you develop discernment skills, you can be prone to believe whatever you hear or read. Insincere people can certainly sound honest, can't they? It doesn't mean that they are; you already know that the "news" is not really factual! Some Communicators also develop their own diversion tactics. Able to convince others persuasively, it can be easy to become manipulative. Still other Communicators become scared of speaking or writing truth and shut down, preferring to hide in the woodwork or re-fuse to share their opinions in case others might disagree or re-spond with anger. In relation to finances, you must express your-self to be heard. Read the right reports to make a solid financial decision and say "no" to the wrong jobs or financial "opportuni-ties." Courage balances out the fifth chakra Communicator.

Success tips: Use your communication skills! If in doubt, get on the phone and ask someone about an investment, a job, or an op-portunity. You're unhappy with a financial adviser, investment, or a purchase? Write a letter or call the company's president. Worse case scenario, write a letter to the editor of your local paper. Other tips include:

- Research corporate materials and information to inves-tigate a company. Then get on the phone and talk with someone.
- You'll prosper best with investments or businesses that are communication in orientation. Anything that links people for communicative purposes just makes sense—and cents—to you.
- Use your verbally oriented intuitive skills to read be-tween the lines when combing through annual reports or evaluating financial opportunities. Trust your instinct.
- Ask the Divine to provide you words when you need them, especially when dealing with big money, such as a home purchase or a new job.
- Consider working in communications of any sort, from sales to public relations. Music, speaking, writing, and other types of communications arenas are also perfect for you. You're a natural. If you're a homemaker, volunteer in communications activities to hone professional skills.
- As a channel for information, some communiqués will come straight from the Divine, others from God-approved sources, and others from less than preferable

sources. If you keep getting bad advice from living or invisible sources, consider issues stemming from the ages of 6½ and 8½, the years in which communication suddenly excels in importance. Were you listened to? Were your ideas valued? Did you know how to express yourself? Were your no's taken as no's, and your yes's as such? What "old tapes" might you be replaying? Address these issues, preferably with a professional, and clear your communication channels.

Dealing with debt and financial problems:

- Get on the phone and talk with your creditors. You are believable. Use your listening skills to probe for the bottom line and then work out a deal.
- If you're innocent of a financial debt or falsely held accountable for money you didn't spend, use your communication savvy to deal with the situation. Write everything down. Obtain supportive documentation. Get others to speak for you. Get the highest official possible to help you.
- While you're not as analytical as a third chakra person, you can read a budget, accounts receivable, or bank statement. Keep up on your accounting. You're perfectly capable of it and in a pinch, you can catch mistakes.
- Sometimes, your honesty can get you in trouble. In case of a suit, consult with a lawyer before you start responding or talking. You want to frame your involvement in a situation in a positive light without lying. A lawyer can help do that.

Methods for decision making:

- Use your verbal intuition to ask for spiritual input. Ask to literally hear an answer from God as you understand God when in daily life or through your dream life.

- Allow the Divine to speak through other people as well. I encourage those gifted with the fifth chakra to use the "rule of three." If you hear the same statement or advice three times in a short time period, you ought to consider it a sign and pay attention.
- Read and analyze as many financial materials as you can. Talk to people, read, and watch television—follow your communication sources when considering a financial move. Then turn it over to God and ask for a word of advice, such as suggested above.
- Use a friend as a sounding board. It can help to speak your mind out loud. Explain clearly that you don't need feedback as much as you desire an audience. By listening to yourself talk, you'll come up with your own response to a financial question.
- Consider music in any form as a means to clear your mind or relax your body, thus allowing your natural intelligence to peruse a monetary issue. Many fifth chakra Communicators use mantras to establish a mindful state or sing to meditate. They might pray when playing music or compose music or lyrics to read their inner minds. I have a fifth chakra friend who uses toning bowls when stressed to reach a restful state.

Communicators have made sure that their voices have been heard through the centuries, among them Beethoven, Mozart, and Haydn—and numerous other inspirational musical composers. Virginia Woolf and Mary Wollstonecraft Shelley wrote for women's issues. Many Communicators express the need for world change through their gifts. The current Dalai Lama connects his Spiritualist gifts with those of Communicating to speak for the way of peace worldwide, as both Nelson Mandela and Martin Luther King, Jr., have done as well. Princess Diana of England joined her Feeler gifts with her Communication abilities to represent children's needs.

CHAKRA SIX MONEY STYLE: VISIONARY

Style: You are the visionary of the chakra system. Because of this, you heavily rely upon your inner visual senses to make decisions about anything, not just money. When it comes to money, however, you like to follow an actual strategy to achieve financial success. If a financial choice doesn't fit into the "big picture," you'll lose interest. Your overall financial style involves setting long-range goals and following a strategy toward success.

Needs: You need to plan for financial security down the road. You can scrimp today to pay for tomorrow and set aside savings to play in the future. Of all the chakra styles, yours is the best suited for long-range commitments and analysis.

Values: Money in and of itself isn't a key value to you, but success is. You like to set goals and achieve them. If you set financial goals, you won't actually feel successful until you do achieve them—and then, you'll probably suffer a let down. You need goals and a plan to achieve them. Once you've reached the end point, you'll feel like it's all over. In a nutshell, your major values in relation to prosperity are long-term security, goal setting and achievement, and strategic planning.

Drives: You're driven to establish an image of your future self then plow ahead until you become that vision. Basically, you're motivated to create the desired future through financial gain. You're fine moving like a turtle—if you get to end up living like the hare! Regarding monetary success, you'll measure it by the practical achievements that others consider out of reach, including monies in retirement, college, insurance, and nursing-home funds.

Strengths: We all earn money on an accrual basis. If you were to total your ten years earnings, you'd be amazed at your money-making ability. Likewise, the best way to save is by thinking over the long haul. Do you know what happens when you keep doubling five thousand dollars? You have over a million in eight turns! Sixth chakra visionaries are great with moneymaking and management because they see the larger view. Like eagles, they can spot opportunities from afar and can also see potential danger moving in. Therefore, they make smart decisions about when to plunge for the mouse (or gold) and when to hold off. You are the financial planners of the chakra system.

Weaknesses: You can't defer all financial decisions. When offered a job today, you should reply tomorrow. Not every wise financial decision seems, in the moment, to streamline into a lifelong plan. Only hindsight can tell us what was really smart or not. Dedication to the future and the plan can cause a visionary to reject a solid short-term opportunity and lose out in the long run.

Success tips: Your best way to approach money? Tie saving and making money to a meaningful goal, so you can never reach the end of your moneymaking objectives! Other ideas include:

- To deal with your tendency to pack rat all your money for tomorrow or at least a "rainy day," make sure that every time you save for the future, you spend a little money on something you consider worthwhile and facing you today. This will keep you happy yet flexible.
- Teach others how to think long-term. This will help you exercise your own gift and help others.
- Thinking of changing professions to make more money? Remember that you are a visionary. Because of this, you can sell your abilities at long-range thinking, futuring, and creative ideation—the packaging of imaginative ideas for creating the future. Depending upon your other strengths, you can also tie your visioning abilities into any other profession. For instance, a Relater-Visionary could

become a terrific healer, especially if you cultivate your visioning gifts in the form of, say, hypnosis. A Feeler-Visionary is often a good artist or interior designer. Take a Feeler-Visionary-Thinker and you have an architect or engineer, while a Visionary-Communicator is great at marketing and a Manifester-Visionary can do anything from start a business to invent products to serve as a finance expert.

- Good basic careers for any Visionary could include marketing, strategic management, and working in insurance, interior design, or any other visual or long-term concern.
- If you're blocked financially, consider using visual tools to unblock. Hypnosis, guided meditation, and creative visualization can all pinpoint blocks and decrease stress and anxiety. Visionaries excel at using these tools for themselves or others. Mapping can also be useful. Draw pictures or cut them out of a magazine, selecting those that represent your long-range goals. Paste them on cardboard and post your visual plan in your office, bedroom, bathroom, or kitchen, wherever you're most likely to look. You'll respond well to visual planning tools such as these.
- Use your clairvoyance, the innate intuitive ability to gain spiritual insights through your inner eye. Picture where you want to be and what type of person you want to become when setting long-range objectives.
- Your financial blocks might have accrued during the years 8½ to 13, when your visual chakra was activated. During these years, we are all highly affected by cultural standards. If society supported your spiritual view of self, then you'll be eager to work hard and play hard. You'll believe in your own success and deserving of it. If you imprinted negative cultural values, such as those that limited your sense of self, you'll have a hard time driving forward. Your self-image will be so low, it will be hard for

you to accept others' help and God's vision for your life. Examine issues of self-image and self-perception to clear out your financial blocks.

- Want to succeed? See yourself as successful. Learn how to envision the Divine's choices for you, those that enter through the back of this chakra. Assess them in terms of how the Spirit sees you and you'll automatically make successful decisions.

- Creative visualization is an ongoing form of manifesting your desires. Every morning and evening, see yourself successful or having achieved your goal. Continue until you reach this particular goal.

- Again on the more spiritual front, remember that when setting a goal you must seek meaning as the product not the byproduct. Don't make money the actual goal or you'll become disillusioned. It really won't buy happiness. REALLY!

Dealing with debt and financial problems: Despite the best-laid plans, a train sometimes derails. Sometimes it's the conductor's fault, but just as often the track went awry through natural wear and tear. The most important idea for Visionaries with financial woes to remember is this: don't blame yourself. Even if it's your fault, don't blame yourself. Shame is a form of blame. Shame says, "I'm a bad person." Because you're so good at seeing connections, you're prone to internalize the false belief of being bad, rather than simply being a human being who errs. Stay away from shame and you'll be better able to apply your great problem-solving skills and plan your way out. Ways to do this include:

- Projecting into the future. This problem won't stay around forever. Nothing does. It either changes or changes you. If it changes you, you've adapted and the problem isn't the same anymore. Select a time frame in which you can reasonably expect clear sailing. Imagine your life at that time and ask yourself how you fixed your financial situation or how it was fixed. Now build a plan backward, applying this future knowledge to the here and now.

- Despite your own futuring skills, you can sometimes lack the knowledge to see your way through today's issues. Get a good legal or accounting adviser, find out your options, then create your plan.
- Change the means of meeting your objectives. If you planned on retiring on Enron money, you're out of luck. You might have to scale down your investment ideas and plan on working longer. Grieve the future you envisioned then ask yourself what you really liked about your original plan. Keep these elements and forge new paths to the same basic objectives. For instance, if you planned on using Enron money to buy a sailboat to sail around the world, why not now learn how to sail then get a paid job on a cruise ship?
- Seek help from others for short-term solutions. You might not think of them, as you are so long-term.

Methods for decision making:

- Want to decide on a good investment? Ask the Divine for the revelation or pictures that will tell you what to do and trust any insights received. As with all visualizations, if the picture isn't clear or doesn't make sense, ask for another one until you've gained complete understanding.
- Use guided meditation. Get quiet and calm and then ask your inner wisdom or the Divine for a picture to solve a particular financial problem or to impart financial wisdom.
- Try guided imagery. Guided imagery requires a partner, who helps you relax then tells you to imagine yourself in a secluded, safe spot. Your partner now invites a guide to appear before you. You can assure the safety of this guide by

asking that God send you the appropriate messenger. You may now ask this guide questions about your situation. If you'd rather, have your partner ask the guide your questions, then record your guide's answers as you repeat them.

- Use futuring. In futuring, you project yourself forward to see how you've solved a problem or to set achievable goals. You can either select a certain time frame, such as futuring forward ten years, or project visually into a solution, such as viewing the time in which a certain problem is solved.
- Ask for a dream. Dream visions can often help us unlock our inner wisdom or link us with spiritual guidance.
- When seeking to select between two choices, vision the outcome of either path. What will your future look like if you buy the house on Queen Avenue? Or the house on Prairie Street? Though the future isn't set, you can see trends and tendencies.

All great leaders have either been Visionaries or been supported by them. For example, "I Have a Dream" is the most famous speech of Reverend Martin Luther King, Jr., an acclaimed Spiritualist-Communicator. By repeating a refrain from a popular Black spiritual folksong, King expressed a compelling alternative vision of social life in America. Thomas Jefferson and his peers created America based on a new political vision, as Lenin did in the Soviet Union. Adolf Hitler illustrates the power of dark visions. The dream-visions of the Hebrew Joseph of the Bible earned him leadership in ancient Egypt. Susan B. Anthony's vision got the women in America the vote, while Golda Meir of Israel helped change some fundamental ideas while she served as Prime Minister.

CHAKRA SEVEN MONEY STYLE: SPIRITUALIST

Style: As you've probably guessed by now, there's your own idea for your life—and the Divine's. When you fall short of your spiritual ideals, life simply doesn't work as well. As the most spiritual of the chakra types it will be impossible, absolutely impossible, for you to make lasting money at anything that you don't believe in. And it will be impossible for you to deal with life until you figure out what "God" means to you.

To be spiritual means to be "filled by the spirit." As a seventh chakra specialist, you are highly attuned to differentiating between the things, people, and opportunities invested with the Spirit and those that are not. This doesn't mean you're perfect at telling the difference or even living the difference all the time. Because we're here to learn unconditional love, you have to start with yourself—by offering yourself unconditional forgiveness and grace at not being as perfect as you think that you can be!

Having said this, you'll do best financially if you follow the program. The Divine's program, that is. Otherwise, your guilt at money ill-gained will eat you up, though you'll probably self-sabotage your success and lose any "bad money" before you waste away. Look for your spiritual calling or let it come to you. Follow it and you'll be financially secure and even affluent. Consider Abraham, the founder of Judaism, Christianity, and Islam. Do you have any idea how many goats the guy had? He was a seventh chakra Spiritalist and he did amazingly well on the financial front!

Needs: You don't actually need money. In fact, the most animated Spiritualists tend to reject money in favor of what they believe to be God's favor. Monks, nuns, and other ascetics number in this crowd. Your strongest need is to "earn" Divine favor, which is impossible! Divine love is freely given. You do, however, have to earn money to buy the basics. Put your spiritual purpose first and your needs will be supplied.

Values: Your values are spiritual, like hope, truth, faith, love, and grace. These are to be acclaimed and are treasures in and of themselves. While you might not value money, you can certainly see how money can help you bring hope to the needy, print words that hold truth, increase faith among the desperate, buy food cooked with love, and deliver grace to the unfortunate. Accept money not as a necessary evil but as a loving gesture of spiritual values.

Drives: You are driven to bring more heaven on earth. Your means of doing this is to act as a prophet, someone who interprets the Spirit's desires to others. The Divine shares the divine with you, and you inform the rest of us.

If someone is on a path of doom, you'll know it—and feel driven to tell her so. If a company is unethical, you'll picket a Board of Management meeting until someone will listen to you. Being a prophet is a hard job. People don't always want to hear the truth, and you don't always want to tell them the truth. But you must and so you do. Money isn't a driving force, but it can help to drive the spiritual forces unto earth.

Strengths: You are connected to the Divine and the spiritual realms and, because of this, can automatically sense what the Above might want you or others to do to achieve divine destiny. You'll know which companies might aim at a spiritual future and which ones don't. Consequently, you'll know how to invest your money ethically. On the moneymaking front, you'll also be able to accurately read which employers are mission and values oriented and which ones are not. As long as you work for an organization that furthers spiritual grace, you will be able to work hard, be a great employee, and receive ample rewards.

Weaknesses: If unethical or dishonest individuals surround you, you'll stop being productive. This doesn't work well if you're, say, a corporate communications specialist. If you're working for an organization that's doing something dirty, you might subtly sabotage the company or yourself. Your bathroom might already be plastered with job-releasing pink slips! Your value system can be your undoing.

Many Spiritualists think that money is evil so they don't save any. How ethical is it to live off other people or the welfare system if you refuse to participate in this errant world? Spiritualists can easily make the mistake of being judgmental instead of values driven. Acting better than others won't increase your popularity and could cost you—not just money, but marriages and friendships. While you don't have to keep your ethics to yourself, remember it's better to wear them than to say them.

Success tips: Hitch your wagon to a star and you can fly far! Excuse the poor rhyme but in your case, Spiritualist, it's really true. It's vital that you follow your spiritual calling, which will involve helpings others "find God," as the Divine desires to be found by them. Specific ideas include:

- In selecting a moneymaking profession, put your values and spiritual calling foremost. Deal with resistance to getting paid and rewarded, and follow your dreams.
- Looking for a career? Consider spiritual, ministerial, counseling, or consulting professions, if you're a strong Spiritualist. No matter your specific profession, you'll quickly become a pastor to the flock, a values-based listener and teacher who can help others figure out themselves. For instance, the best career counselors are Spiritualists because they're good at figuring out others' spiritual destinies.
- Only, only, only work for organizations or concerns that mirror your values. Otherwise, you'll fail.
- If you can't find an organization that suits you, start your own. There are thousands of independent business people in every industry that are Spiritualist. You can sell widgets or Bibles; it doesn't matter because to you, it's how you touch people that counts.
- Look to the bigger picture to solve values conflicts. Your

greatest challenge could involve perceiving an ethical conflict where perhaps there isn't one. Let's say, for instance, you feel called to the ministry at a pay scale of one dollar to the ten you're now making. You need the ten rather than one, however, because you have a family to support. Be responsible. Stick with your current responsibilities but add volunteer work or an avocation, then plan for your future. I know many couples that raise their children then join a ministerial team, the Peace Corps, an international medical community, or teach English in a foreign language after they've "retired."

• Regarding investment, you might be tempted to give all your money to your church or synagogue—sometimes when your son really needs it for sneakers. You might think it's nobler to invest in the Red Cross than in your daughter's soccer team or, certainly, than in a 401K plan with questionable pursuits. Don't let your attitude disappoint your moth-eaten wallet or your money-hungry mother-in-law. First, peruse investments that are socially or religiously responsible. There are lots of them and there are financial counselors who can consult with you. Second, consider investing in yourself, either starting your own ethical business or ministry service. If you lack a strong financially oriented chakra, either partner or seek assistance with payroll, salary and savings, legal, and ownership/ equity issues.

• If you have blocks to financial success, consider examining your religious beliefs. Religion and spirituality can be very different. Religious dogma can sometimes stunt your growth or success. Also review what happened during years 13 and 21, those involving your seventh chakra. If you weren't supported in finding your personal and spiritually ordained life mission, or if you were blocked in healing earlier life problems, you won't think you deserve success. You won't feel worthy in the eyes of the Divine.

You might even think it's bad or evil to make money. If these are the types of beliefs stopping you from succeeding, take a look at history. The Spirit rewards those who follow. Make the hard decisions you might need to make to get on a "prosperity path."

Dealing with debt and financial problems: For obvious, or maybe unobvious, reasons, Spiritualists are often one of the most likely chakra styles to go into debt or make too little money. Beliefs, personal views, and shame might prevent you from meeting your monetary needs. If you flounder and go into debt or can't make a living, consider the following:

- Examine your spiritual beliefs against authentic Scripture. There's evidence in all sound spiritually based religions that God wants you to be successful.
- Work with a commonsense spiritual adviser or spiritually oriented therapist to better understand and clear your beliefs in lack and limitation.
- Hire financial help. Select a professional who shares your viewpoints to get the assistance you need. Don't feel embarrassed about needing others—don't other people need you?
- Go bankrupt if you need to do so. I know that both Judaism and Christianity underscore the need for forgiveness of debts, as do other religions. Do what you need to do and then create a more authentic plan moving forward.
- Get a second job. In fact, do your vocation in your spare time and get a paying job for full-time! Providing for yourself and your loved ones IS moral.
- Charge money for your services. No one can afford to give him or herself away, even you. I often tell Spiritualists that they aren't charging for spiritual energy, but for their own personal time.
- Forgive yourself. You're human.

• Pledge a certain amount of your earnings to a good cause.
It will help you feel ethical making more money.

Methods for decision making: Always return to your core values.
From there, there are three main ways to engage your spiritual
self or God in your decisions.

1. Prayer: Sending messages to the Divine or Divinely ap-
   proved sources. There is silent prayer, involving internal
   discussion; active prayer, in which you ask for spiritual
   messages while you exercise, move, or entertain your
   daily life; petitioning prayer, in which you ask for what
   you need, then wait; intercessory prayer, where you re-
   quest someone else to pray for you; and eternal prayer, in
   which you state your needs and then forget about them.
2. Meditation: Receiving messages from the Divine. You can
   meditate quietly or throughout your day, taking a few
   moments for peace and quiet. Some people clear their
   minds, others repeat a mantra, play music, or repeat a
   repetitive phrase as when using prayer beads. Do what
   works for you.
3. Contemplation: Communion with your God source.
   When contemplating, you are basking in the presence of
   the Holy. Some people do this through prayer or meditation, but contemplation can also be much simpler in
   that it doesn't involve setting an intention. Simply being
   in union with the Divine can invite awareness, financial
   or otherwise.

Spiritualists have changed the world since time began. We
could actually count Greek philosopher Socrates and his student
Plato in our numbering, as both peered behind the veil for truth.
Both Catherine and Francis of Assisi stand out in the Christian
count, as does Confucius, Rumi, and the Buddha in other parts
of the world. Contemporary Spiritualists include world-famous
Reverend Billy Graham.

Chakra Eight Money Style: Shaman

Style: For you, it's all about power. Money isn't about skill or healing, building, or helping. It's about having and wielding power. Eighth chakra individuals are the power hungry, power makers of the world.

But there's more to having power than meets the eye. Money is power, and power is used for mystical reasons. To the Shaman, the source of all power and powers lies in the mystical planes. You can use this power to help, to heal, or to hurt and injure. The decision is personal.

As a Shaman, you are specially equipped to "walk between the worlds," to link the natural, human, energetic, and spiritual domains with your very body. You are skilled at such linkages. Each time you connect someone with a different time or space, a plant with a sick person, or a planet with a prediction, you gain an extra boost of voltage: you become more powerful. Shamans in touch with their mystical abilities can easily become successful at being powerful and therefore use power to make money—and in turn, use money to purchase more power. Using power for your own gain isn't the way to make friends. Using your power to empower others, however, produces more personal power—and in the end, more wealth!

Needs: Your strongest need is for power because power gets things done. Power is the force that moves mountains, heals tumors, and accesses divine inspiration. As Spiritualists have long said, if you pray powerfully you receive powerful answers. Shamans understand the vitality of power and long to gain this power so they can create substantial change.

Values: Power isn't truly a value. It is a shamanic need but not a value. Values are ideals that are chosen to increase or decrease our godliness. Shamans don't have values. I mean this: By nature, the Shaman understands that there is equal strength and correctness to both sides of a duality. There are times when acting good can be bad, and when acting bad can be good. Therefore the Shaman is original among chakra types in being able to choose from the entire grab bag of human and divine choices to simply do what works. The Shaman, therefore, doesn't value what we call values, but prizes outcomes.

Drives: The Shaman is driven to gain power but always in order to achieve a higher purpose, the purpose being mystical. Mysticism is the unfolding of the mysterious to the known. On the other hand, mysticism is also delivering the known to the Great Mystery. The Shaman puzzles and can be puzzling because he or she is driven toward a pursuit none other can see. The drive for money can totally consume a Shaman, and yet, a true Shaman can in a blink, turn around and give away all this hard-acquired income with no care or thought as to the cost of acquisition.

Strengths: Because the Shaman lives in the seams between the worlds, holding nothing as more sacred or profane than anything else, he or she can truly see into the heart of a matter, the substance of an illusion or the truth of a lie. Shamans can see why someone else wants to make money. Shamans can read the intent behind an annual report, an employer, or an employee. Shamans can stand away and allow a financial disaster to occur, if that person knows that only through disaster can something higher be created. For instance, a shamanic parent might let her son drive his company into the hole, knowing that this is the only way he will learn how to be humble rather than arrogant.

Weaknesses: Access through the illusion can lead to believing that we control the illusion. In a world where black and white are the same, it's all too easy to think that we are masters of matter and also have the right to do anything we want. Ego, arrogance, cruelty, and petty jealousy often affect Shamans, turning them from magicians of spirit to black magicians, those who steal energy from others for their own ends. A black magician is the same with money as with people. Greedy, selfish, and controlling, Black Shamans use money to gain and wield power no matter what. Those with money and shamanic abilities have perpetuated the worst crimes of the world. Ironically, the same can be said of Shamans without money or power. Wife or child abusers, for instance, are often strong in shamanism; ironically, some have often been abused as well. Abused Shamans of any age need to realize that their power is being stolen and to take measures to "get it back" and become intact.

Success tips: The best way for Shamans to look at money is through the eye of mythology. In Greek story time, the River of Death is rowed by Charon, who collects a coin before agreeing to take you from the embankment of life to the beaches of death. Shamans are like Charon. They collect a coin before assisting a client, a corporation, or even a personal investment. Remember that the point isn't the money. It's the transformational process you as Shaman conduct. You help others move from a set point through a change process to an established outcome. While good and bad aren't in a Shaman's vocabulary, ethics are.

Money doesn't always have to be the exchange. Energy must balance. You don't want to tip the balance between people or the worlds. In exchange for your assistance, you can also accept gratitude, learning, or a dividend. Here are some of the quirky yet very real tips that will work for the Shaman seeking money in an ethical way:

- Seek energy exchanges rather than just money. You know that if energy is taken from one plane of existence without being returned, the universe tilts. If you give without receiving, all of life goes out of balance. Money isn't the only means of receiving when you've given. But do accept if it's provided.
- Continue defining money as a means of power. Instead of purchasing power with your money, however, purchase healing or wholesome deeds for self and other. Your

abundance will overflow as positive energy attracts positive energy.

- Along the same lines, use your power to help empower others. Being the leader instead of the teacher increases others' self-confidence.
- Seek investments (or investors) that need your help. Your ability to move energy and move between the worlds can "heal" a company in distress and make you money as that company turns around.
- Use with caution your ability to remote view, or leave the body, to see into other realities. Everything done in the world produces an equal effect. If you project your sight into a corporate meeting to gain undisclosed secrets, someone will do the same to you—except it might be into the bedroom! Karma, the law of returns, affects Shamans.
- Know that it's ethical to use your ability to connect worlds and perform energy transformation and healing to create money for yourself and others. You have command of all the chakras' intuitive abilities. You can use the other chakras to perform these functions:

1. Use first chakra manifestation or physical sympathy to sense what's going on in the physical world.
2. Enable second chakra feeling sympathy or the sensing of others' emotions to create compassion for others.
3. Connect with third chakra analysis or gut instinct to gather data.
4. Access healing energies through the fourth chakra to make a positive difference.
5. Direct fifth chakra communication skills to hear what spiritual guides or the Divine has to say.
6. Use the sixth chakra to peer into possible futures.
7. Allow seventh chakra spiritual attunement to help you consult God for the Divine plan.
8. Journey through the fourth chakra for lucid dreaming and to access various dimensions and planes of

existence. You can also do this directly through your eighth chakra.

9. Read ninth chakra soul awarenesses to break old patterns and establish new ones.
10. Apply tenth chakra natural sensitivities to call on the environment for helpers, information, and healing energies.
11. Command abundance or moneymaking opportunities through your eleventh chakra.

You have a lot of gifts at your disposal, for wealth or dispersement of wealth!

- Learn your lessons from the past. As a Shaman, you can read the Akashic Records, the history annals of time containing everything you or someone else has ever done, said, or thought. Want to avoid mistakes you made a long time ago? Read about them—and learn!
- Are you financially blocked? Many powerful Shamans actually have a resistance to success. Usually, this is because they are afraid of their own power, thinking that they're going to hurt others with their energy. These sorts of false beliefs usually lie in the past, even in former lives. First, forgive yourself for your past mistakes. Second, forgive others. From an energetic viewpoint, forgiving others involves offering Divine energy to offenders. The guilty can decide to accept the transformational energy or not. If they do, they are transfigured and moved out of your life and space. If they do not, Divine energy pushes them from you so you can't be harmed anymore. Some characters don't learn and continue to attempt evil. The "white" energy of Divinity simply deflects the "black" energy of the evildoer back to them. You're safe. They're not.

Dealing with debt and financial problems: At a subtle level, Shamans might get into debt because they know that they can get out of it.

Magic is real, as is the summoning of power to produce effect. But you know, it's a lot of work to keep climbing in and out of financial straits. You might want to decide to simply stay solvent.

Having said this, let's say you're in debt or have money problems, such as inability to make decent money. There are two basic shamanic means for dealing with this:

1. Make more money. As a Shaman, you have full command of the psychic senses. Use these in your world. Charge for your services. Are you a real estate agent? Seek an unusual, contrarian population to assist, such as individuals with no money—or the super-rich. Are you in business? Offer futuring or dream services for decision making. Are you an artist? Ask a rich investor to sponsor you; promise that you'll paint paintings of his or her future success and thereby help create it. Be a shaman and you'll be rewarded.

2. Get real and create a payback plan. While you flow opposite, the world doesn't. Honestly and truly indulge yourself. Hire a financial or career counselor and create a long-term plan for debt repayment, bankruptcy, or moneymaking. You must use someone who understands the unusual, that you are unusual, and can help you sculpt a splashy path through life.

Methods for decision making: Review the "Success tips" for the list of all the mystical means available to make decisions. Regarding investment decisions, you're best sticking with first, third, fifth, sixth, and seventh chakra gifts. Regarding career options, you must add the second and fourth chakras, because what you do will affect other people. For selecting a home, geographic location, or real estate, use your first or tenth chakra abilities, especially the tenth. Shamans are better off in the natural, even if your only option is to decorate a city apartment with plants and skins!

If you tend toward the unethical or manipulative use of power or money, develop a code of ethics. And stick to it.

Shamans can sometimes be found in unexpected places. One of the most well-known is author Carlos Castaneda, who reintroduced the world to the shamanic during the 1970s and 80s. Then we have Ronald Reagan—yes, I mean this!—the actor-turned-president. Want to know a Shamanic director? Alfred Hitchcock! Successful female shamans include Leona Helmsley of the Helmsley Hotel chains and Mary Magdalene of Biblical times. And of course, there's Jesus Christ.

Chakra Nine Money Style: Idealist

Style: Does money really make the world go around? You know that it doesn't. Goodness does.

You are one of the world's harmonizers. As such, you're about making sure that people help people and that money supports people helping people. To say that money is unimportant would be going too far. Yes, it's important, as long as it's being used for a good and just cause, one that makes the world go around. You're an idealist and as such are one of the social justice harbingers of society. It's all about causes: world peace, world hunger, and save the whales—and anything and everything else that needs to be saved. Regarding your money style, you know that it takes money to save the world. Your greatest financial gift is therefore getting money out of people for a good reason: It's called exhortation. Unlike the Mafia, you exhort for goodness not greed!

Needs: You'll have a hard time putting your needs before others, because there's always someone with greater needs than you have. Want to spend your hard-earned money on a muffin? Whoops—there's a street person who can't afford a piece of bread, much less a muffin. There goes that Starbucks coffee, too. If you want to be really honest, you need to be needed and to feel like you make a difference. That's your bottom-line.

Values: While the Spiritualist esteems values themselves, you value ideals that have a practical application. If a Spiritualist idealizes faith, an Idealist supports faith in justice. If a Spiritualist upholds honesty, you'll insist upon honesty against dishonest politicians. You value social change and are willing to sacrifice for it.

Drives: You are driven to change the world, one person, community, or cause at a time. Why else are we here?

Strengths: You are either a good natural leader or follower, depending upon your other chakra strengths. If accompanied by a strong will-based chakra, such as the first or eighth, you can lead a social movement. If your supportive chakras are softer, such as second or fourth, you might be a follower and a very important one at that. You might minister to your fellow change agents, not just the individuals you're helping. If the fifth or third chakra accompanies your ninth, you could be a good instructor, organizer, or teacher.

You're probably very good at explaining a cause, raising capital and resources, and obtaining people support. A lesser-known strength is your ability to perceive patterns.

A powerful Idealist sees patterns in him or herself and in the world. Patterns are created within the soul, the part of the self that moves through time and space and holds memory. Idealists can read souls, interpret the true nature of others, figure out the meaning of difficult times, and define the destiny of humankind and others. In other words, an Idealist can see what's keeping us stuck and what will move us onto a more spiritualized path.

This strength is an asset in problem solving, fundraising and development, organizational leadership, professorial teaching, philosophizing, ethics management, and personal consulting and counseling, all ideal professions for a straightforward Idealist.

Weaknesses: The other side of idealism is cynicism. Who hasn't experienced the dashing of dreams, the disappointment of failure, and the difficulties of cowardice? People will let you down, as will systems and procedures. Seeing the best in other's souls can lead to believing that people will act accordingly. That's not human nature. Striving for the ideal must include the acceptance of the humanness of humanity, or you will pull yourself out of society altogether. If you're not in the system, you won't make any money.

You might also lack financial resources or savings because you give away all your money. As a natural fundraiser, you can explain a cause to just about anyone. The trouble is, it can be hard to see yourself as a just cause. Sure, we all need to eat but . . . think of those starving kids in India!

Success tips: Find a good cause, lead or follow, and make sure you "tithe" or apportion a meaningful part of the earnings to yourself. See yourself as a good cause, too! Other pointers are:

- Blocked from meeting your own financial needs? Consider examining issues lying within your soul and your concept of reality. If you can see that prosperity actually helps you achieve a larger end and your own soul purpose, you will allow abundance into your own life.
- Frankly, you can make your own money by inventing products or services that serve social justice.
- Link your ninth chakra to another chakra. I often find Idealists flounder when it comes to grounding their ideas in reality. By connecting to another gift, you can choose a profession and be an Idealist within a context, a do-gooder with a paycheck. Ideas include:

  1. First chakra: Start a business or make products that serve a higher cause.
  2. Second chakra: Become a counselor, a therapist, or an artist. Work with a population that really needs you, or portray social issues through your art.
  3. Third chakra: Administrate for a nonprofit or organization you admire.

4. Fourth chakra: Become a healer or work in the healing professions.
5. Fifth chakra: Teach or become a communicator, instructing in principles that fit your personality.
6. Sixth chakra: Lead an organization, family, or cause.
7. Seventh chakra: Consider doing missions work of any sort, or offer career or spiritual counseling. If you are also a Communicator, head-hunting would work, too. If you're high in the third chakra, you could also become a management consultant.
8. Eighth chakra: Be a Shaman. Honestly. And charge for your time.
9. Tenth chakra: Invest in land or real estate; be a forester or work in nature; become an herbalist or farmer; live, be on or develop the land, plants or animals. Depending upon your other gifts, consider naturopathy or natural care medicine.
10. Eleventh chakra: Serve in a commanding, leadership position for a worthy organization.

Dealing with debt and financial problems: You tend to give yourself and money away, and this can backfire. If you continue this path, you'll need handouts! To avoid financial woes, get a good financial planner and set goals. If you must, have a friend, loved one, employer, or accountant manage your money and make sure you're budgeting for your own and family needs.

If you're actually buried in creditor's claims, consult an accountant or business professional. If you have to, claim bankruptcy and then set up a long-term, practical plan that includes how to make more money with your gifts. Some Idealists become addicted to fundraising, which can be annoying to others. If your only source of income is hitting up friends, get therapeutic help. As strong as this statement is, you're close to being a gambler. You might need support to just get a regular job and be a regular Joe or Jane until you master the art of fitting in. Look at your own patterns honestly and you'll be able to work through your problems.

Methods for decision making: In any matter, consider what ideal is being served. You'll only prosper if you believe in what you're doing. This decision making is very internal and "soulfully" your own. Want to make a good investment? Invest in companies that represent or follow causes that are meaningful to you. Many Idealists consider investments comparable to donating money and time. After all, you think, you're investing in an ideal, aren't you? If you've gone so far as to give away a lot of time or money to a certain organization, consider working for that organization. That way, everyone wins.

Idealists have made a significant difference in history, often blending their idealism with other chakra skills. Consider Gandhi, the Indian peace activist and nonviolence practitioner; Margaret Thatcher, the British Prime Minister; and John Locke, the English writer whose theories underlie American government.

CHAKRA TEN MONEY STYLE: NATURALIST

Style: Ah, the Birkenstock expert! If your generation was into these natural shoes, you know what I mean. A little younger? Let's try words like organic, free-range, all cotton, and environmentally friendly. You're the chakra type that doesn't often find yourself far away from home unless, of course, you're to be found in the middle of the Amazonian jungle, on an African safari, or on a Siberian skiing expedition.

You are the most natural of all the chakra types. You know that trees don't just stand there; they actually listen to the wind! Flowers don't just bloom, they talk. Birds don't just nest, they deliver omens. Intuitively, you are environmentally sensitive and, like the Shaman, able to perceive messages from nature. Through your connection to the environment, you also maintain the link to all who walked the earth previously. You know that the ancestors are still animate, that genealogy often determines the present, and that what has gone before will come again. Your link to heritage is also a connection to spirits, quick and dead, that can inhabit your world. And because the natural is your world, you have a hard time thinking of money as real.

Unless, of course, you can touch it.

Money makes no sense to you unless it can be used naturally. To really understand money, you must be able to hold it in your hand. This dollar purchases so many oats, and this ten-spot will support ten birds with seed. Your money style? Money won't matter unless it's part of the earth.

Needs: Like the first chakra Manifester, you're vitally aware of primary needs: clothing, air, water, touch, food, and shelter. Obtaining these needs will occupy much of your time, as will tending to natural life, including plants, animals and other living beings, and the land. Money is a means to meeting your primary needs—with a qualifier, as suggested below.

Values: You qualify all your needs with the adjective "natural," requiring that you use environmentally safe substances that don't pollute the earth. Valuing the natural, you also tend toward the historical, the framework of the world.

While Naturalists can be found serving on community preservation committees and local historical societies, researching genealogy, running bird shows or observatories, leading walking groups, selling organic produce or participating in just about anything else connected to the earth or sky, they don't reject money as do the Spiritualists. Like a Spiritualist, however, they don't understand why others see money as the end-all, be-all. After all, it's not real or alive.

Drives: You will feel driven toward environmental causes and to satisfy nature's needs. Because of this, your fiscal intentions will involve making money to invest in your home, nature, the land, healthy food and water, chemical-free clothing, and other sound and tangible products. You're not frugal if you have money and will probably indulge in travels to places environmentally interesting, ancestral, or historical. You are driven to understand and support the natural and genealogical, and that is what you'll do with your money.

Strengths: In touch with the natural, you often speak for it. You're an incredibly important asset for any community, land planning group, or living being with your sensitivity to environmental issues. Cities are functional, but nature is necessary. Your ability to tune into the land, plants, animals, planet, stars, and heavenly bodies assures continuity between humanity and earthly surroundings. You're also extremely profitable at any business, activist campaign, or non-profit endeavor regarding primary human needs or nature, as long as these activities are healthy for all.

Weaknesses: Sometimes, its healthier to use chemical or human-made substances rather than organic ones. A Naturalist might reject a medicine that could save his or her life if it was developed with animal testing or contains a synthetic agent. As well, human expansion sometimes involves the destruction of nature. A Naturalist can be so natural that he or she can fail to see the need for balance and negotiation. This tendency will carry into a Naturalist's personal finances, potentially creating a rebellious spirit against things human, such as money. Many Naturalists live figuratively on air—not a solid commodity when it comes to paying for the environmentally pure home they've built in the woods! Rigidity might feel ethical, but it ultimately undoes the Naturalist if taken too far.

Success tips: Look for career and investment opportunities in, well, your own backyard! Truly, look to the natural for making money and nature will reward you. Specifics include:

- Select natural or genealogically oriented careers, including forestry, land development, real estate, archeology, anthropology, feng shui consulting, environmental sciences, astronomy, astrology, natural medicine, farming, herbology, landscaping, log home building, construction, lumbering, ley line tracking (natural energy lines in the earth that create electromagnetic charges), commodities brokering, dog walking, animal raising or management, cooking or catering, corporate work in agriculture, producing organic products of any sort, gardening, historical research or teaching, travel agent or travel guide, veterinarian . . . you get the picture!

- Buy only natural products for yourself and your family, and you'll be healthier. Naturalists are prone to be environmentally sensitive and allergic to chemicals.
- Better yet, start a business making or distributing natural products. You'd be a natural!
- Deal in cash. When at all possible, pay your bills through automatic checking account withdrawals and do your day-to-day interactions with cash. Invisible money doesn't exist for you, so you're not great at budgeting unless you're actually holding money in your hand.
- If at all possible, don't use credit cards. They aren't real to you, and you could easily rack up very real bills.
- If you're questioning a career move, go back to school to update your resume before switching professions. There are many certificates and degrees that support the Naturalist and can be put to work.
- Regarding investments, look to long-range investment opportunities that are health conscious, such as socially responsible mutual funds. Buy stocks in companies that manufacture or distribute natural products, such as fuel cells or organic cotton shirts. Personalize your investments by spending the extra money to buy land and build environmentally safe homes or houses. There are Naturalists out there who will purchase from you later!
- Analyze any resistance to success for the following reasons.

First, ancestral interference. If you are connected to a negative entity or thought form from the past, you might suffer financial inhibition. Second, your own history. By clearing out your misguided beliefs, you will clear out your resistance to prosperity. Third, question if you're living in accordance with your values. You are nature based. If you're spending money on chemical-laden food, artificial fertilizer, or plastic clothing, your innate sensibilities could reject the money used to obtain these products. Go natural and get richer. If these reasons don't fit, ask yourself if you are in synch with your purpose. You are a natural-based healer. Your best ways to make money are to use natural products and resources to soothe and assist your fellow human beings or beings in nature.

Dealing with debt and financial problems: Naturalists can be antagonistic to money or wealth. It's just that the intangible seems so impractical, you can actually develop impractical spending patterns! As suggested under "Success tips": see a financial counselor and immediately convert to a cash-basis system.

Consider the following:

- Get a friend or appropriate financial expert to review your assets, if you own land or a home. Naturalists don't always know the true value of their holdings. They feel emotions not dollar signs when dealing with land, houses, furniture, and other shelter-based assets.
- Having obtained an asset statement, get help in conducting a debt assessment and a budget. Bear with the process.
- If you're in financial trouble (which your creditors might already be insisting,) work with a debt consolidator, bankruptcy expert, or other individual to get on track.
- If you have stock, real estate, or mutual fund investments,

consider converting them to a socially responsible source. You'll feel better and therefore achieve greater success.

- Declutter. If you're in confusion, get rid of the clutter in your life and your mind will clear. Apply feng shui or other energy-balancing processes to change your home and personal energy.
- Move your furniture. You'll think differently and see new opportunities in old places.
- Travel. Get out of town and you'll see your problems a different way.
- Begin a second job making money at following your ethics. Start a catering business. Or how about an organic farming operation? Research genealogy or start a scrapbook-making business. Sell your arts and crafts at shows. Get a real estate license and add a little feng shui. You'll be surprised at how successful you'll be!

Methods for decision making: Look to nature and nature will take care of you. Environmental intuitives can often receive and send messages to the world of nature and both prosper accordingly. Consider:

- Asking God to send you an omen, message, sign, or warning through the natural. Study the meaning of various natural phenomena to interpret these responses.
- Going natural when in doubt. Invest, buy, or purchase natural-based endeavors or products.
- Balancing your abhorrence of the synthetic with practical reasoning by consulting a friend who is dissimilar to you.
- Walking around the block when you need to clear your head. You'll think better.

Remember Euell Gibbons? He was a Naturalist who sold cereal years ago! Other Naturalists have made it big, including the legendary Johnny Appleseed of American history, anthropologist Margaret Mead and underseas expert Jacques Cousteau.

CHAKRA ELEVEN MONEY STYLE: COMMANDER

Style: You, of all the chakra types, know exactly what REALLY makes the world go around. Forces. Lots and lots of invisible forces.

As a transmuter and commander of these forces, you can bend the invisible to your will. You will innately be able to sense the presence of the various natural and spiritual energy forces, from gravity and electromagnetic waves to the Spiritual Forces, Virtues, and Rays. If you so desire, you could grab the Force of Abundance from outer space and wrap it to your will, directing it to make money for yourself or others. Compared to marshaling forces, making money can seem dull. But if you put your will to it, you'll be good at it.

Needs: Like your Shaman friend, you don't so much need money as the power that comes with it. Since money is a force creating change in the world, you desire money because of the power that accompanies it.

Values: You value change. You especially value the change that you personally can produce. While your counterpart the Shaman sees no distinction between methods or means to create transformation, you do. You want to match means to outcome. While the Shaman might not care exactly what is left in the wake, you do. You want a clean and clear result with no loose ends. Hence the word "transmuter" applies to you. A Shaman values transformation, a change process leaving waste or unusable materials. A Commander idealizes transmutation, an alchemical process that alters negative wastes into positive gain. Because of this, you will want to squeeze every drop you can out of money or financial investments.

Drives: You are driven to command. You must effect change at will or you will become depressed, negative, moody, and backbiting.

Strengths: Because of your intense abilities, you are the miracle maker of the chakra system. At will, you could learn how to move objects, rearrange atoms, call storms, change the weather, alter patterns, and cure diseases. This ability can transfer straight to finances. Obviously, you can't force a dollar bill to double, but your intensity can benefit a company, employer, or investments. If developed, your intuitive faculties can also enable you to read the power and forces supporting an investment, thereby helping you create successful endeavors.

Weaknesses: Most Commanders struggle with being too forceful or introverted. Arrogance, frustration, and even success can lead to imposing your will on others. This is unethical and even at times evil. Sure, you can force your family or spouse to make money for you and even try to control outcomes, but the results are harmful to you and others in the long run. On the other hand, many Commanders are so afraid of hurting others or being out of "God's will" that they don't use their own Divinely given abilities. They become the victims of the world and can't summon energy to move ahead for the trying.

Success tips: Learn about the natural and spiritual forces making the world go around. My books are a great source for this information, as are books about quantum physics, natural law, and spiritual principles. Then, do the following:

- Apprentice. Connect with a mentor or organization that can teach you how to develop your natural Commanding abilities and guide you into ethical applications. You could consider spiritual, shamanic, intuitive, or healing teachers.
- Consider careers enhanced by your natural inner strengths. The easiest way to select a career from scratch is to look

at your other strong chakras and to use your commanding abilities within those professions. Are you a strong third chakra Thinker? How about getting an MBA, studying forces, and running companies? If your only strong chakra is the eleventh, you might want to consider shamanism or the military as careers. Yes, they are dissimilar paths but they are both about commanding power. One is unstructured and the other is quite structured.

- Never use money as a hold over others. You could be tempted to do this. You won't be liked.
- Instead of using finances to command others, use money to reward individuals when they follow their own paths. A Commander, for instance, can hold money over their kids' heads. "Do what I say, and I'll give you your allowance." That's manipulation with personal will and could damage other people. Instead, suggest that your children select their goals, even in terms of chores. When the goals are met, you kids get an allowance. Now you're supporting others in developing their own personal will.
- Invest in companies or endeavors that are strong and making a potent, positive difference in the world. Your energy will enable further growth for these organizations and yourself.
- When in doubt, consider making your own investments. You'll be able to spot a stock winner and follow it, innately sensing when it's failing or growing.
- If you still don't understand forces after reading a lot of books, then travel. Learn from shamans in various parts of the world.
- Never forget your ability to command the miraculous. Link with God as you understand God and volunteer your time to help the less fortunate. It will do your soul good and your own powers will increase.
- Like the Shaman, your main resistance to success is going to be the idea that money, like power, is evil. Some

transmuters can actually materialize money out of thin air, bending matter as Uri Geller bends spoons. But is it ethical? Is it right? Is it okay to play God—or not? Of course, it's not okay to play God, but neither is it okay to ignore a God-given capability. You are the miracle maker of the chakra system.

In summation, if you as a Commander want to make money, then learn about the ethical use of power and the mystical system of forces. Then learn how to allow success by moving negativity out of power and how to command positive, life-enhancing forces.

Dealing with debt and financial problems: Here are a few pointers.

- Stay out of others' problems. Through sheer will and care, Commanders can too often try and command away others' financial woes. This not only ties up your energy, but also will frustrate you. Ultimately, you can command energy for yourself but others can undo what you do for them if they don't make the internal changes that created their lack of success. You can't permanently change anything or anyone that doesn't want to be healed! Caring Commanders often find themselves in debt for helping others or fixing the world. Don't even try. If you're drowning, you can't help the drowned.
- Keep your finances separate from others' finances. As just explained, you're best able to help yourself and in turn assist those who seek your advice or opinion. In a family situation, consider setting up trusts and doing estate planning. Open different accounts for the various individuals you might provide for.
- Learn the tax laws to keep yourself safe—and to cushion others from your strong and forceful financial moves.
- Separate your own assets. Commanders can be extreme.

You don't want one bad investment to pull down your good investments.

- If you have your own business, make sure you're incorporated so a downswing doesn't affect anything or anyone else.
- Get insurance. You're an extreme personality and could suffer a few mishaps because of it. While you can swing up, you can also dip down.
- If you're in debt, know that you can rebuild. Cut your losses and get financial help to figure out where to throw your energy.

Methods for decision making: By attuning to the world of forces, you will begin to be able to do the following:

- See patterns and make decisions to either follow or escape these patterns.
- Summon natural and spiritual forces at will and use them with other chakra skills to potentially do the following:

  1. First chakra: Look at the practical and material properties involved in a situation. Through this chakra, you can command physical matter at will.
  2. Second chakra: Figure out how you or others might feel if you follow a certain path. You can also determine what emotional blocks might be preventing success.
  3. Third chakra: Check for the spiritual forces creating or preventing structure and organization. Command the forces that will create systems when they are needed.
  4. Fourth chakra: Read your choices for the impact they will have on others. You can also determine which forces are assisting or preventing healthy relationships.
  5. Fifth chakra: You can discern good versus bad sources of verbal or psychic data by checking out the forces

behind a messenger. Then call to yourself a Divinely appointed messenger and the correct forces necessary to implement change.

6. Sixth chakra: Use clairvoyant sight to see potential outcomes regarding your choices or to determine which forces are blocking success or could create success.

7. Seventh chakra: Examine the spiritual forces already imposed upon you. Clear those preventing clear decision making, then ask the Divine to determine which spiritual forces can help you determine choices or create necessary outcomes.

8. Eighth chakra: Walk as the Shaman walks—between worlds—to figure out your choices and to gain spirit-based assistance in implementing your decision.

9. Ninth chakra: Check your soul to conclude which forces are currently in use and for what purpose. Envision the patterns in the present situation and then ask what pattern or outcome is most harmonious for all.

10. Tenth chakra: Learn how to read nature based omens in response to your questions, then apply natural forces through ceremony for manifesting purposes.

Commanders are usually at the top or bottom rung of society's ladder. Want to know who has surfaced to the top? Consider Winston Churchill, whose command of the military made a distinct difference in World War II. Queen Cleopatra of ancient Egypt led men and nations by complementing her Command abilities with her second chakra sensuality and brilliant Thinking mind. Genghis Khan, though a bit violent, is on the same wavelength as Julius Caesar and other Commanders. Uri Geller, the psychic "spoon bender," reflects the energetic abilities of the transmuter. Many spiritual leaders, including Jewish prophets, Christian apostles, Hindu gurus, and Tibetan monks, are known for their phenomenal, commanding feats.

Putting It All Together 5

"I will never wear purple again. Then I thought, No, I won't say never. I don't want any rules. When it comes to numbers and colors, there will be no rules. I'll wear orange and red and pink and sit on that strange blue-black-green couch . . . "[7]

At this point, you should have a good idea of your natural strengths, your chakra-based personality, and your money style. You might also be confused at how to weave these various threads into a workable design for career and financial decision making.

The easiest way to deal with money matters through the chakras is to operate from your strengths. Why select a stock based on its cash-flow statements if you can't read a balance sheet? Why read a balance sheet if you're more interested in creating art objects? It makes more sense to use muscles you have than ones that you don't.

At the same time, you would benefit from assessing and attempting to strengthen your chakric weak spots, if only for your own health. Chakras regulate financial, mental, spiritual, and emotional concerns—but also physical matters! The healthier a chakra, the more robust the connected body functions. While your other chakras can compensate for a weak one, they have to work overtime to deal with what can only be seen as a handicap. I encourage people to "never say never," to never think that a weak chakra is ineffective or useless; rather, it might be a matter of timing and need.

You've been presented with a lot of information, and frankly, you'll have to put a lot of it together yourself. There are thousands of chakra configurations. Think of the geometry of what you've just mapped. While there might be thousands if not millions of individuals with your top one, two, or three chakras, their scores are different, as are the types and scores of their supportive and weaker chakras. Nonetheless, your most effective use of this book is to put together a self-portrait, to tally your chakra strengths, and to determine your true money style. I can't possibly address all configurations and personalize advice, but I will set forth some basics with examples that you can consider.

CONFIGURATION ONE:
IF YOU HAVE ONE STRONG CHAKRA

In many ways, you will have the easiest time dealing with money because your skills and limitations will be very, very obvious, as will the nature of your spiritual self. Other people will be able to describe you to yourself with a great deal of accuracy and can therefore be helpful in providing you feedback or assisting you in building anything from a life to a financial plan.

Take your chakric weaknesses to heart and develop your supportive chakras to compensate. While you can hire or exhort assistance, you'll have to be self-aware or you'll fall into the same financial traps over and over. I'll give you a few examples.

John, a client of mine, is a 50-year-old minister. He is solely a Spiritualist in the Christian tradition, and if he could, would spend all his time doing ministry in the inner city—much to the chagrin of his wife of fourteen years, who finds herself having to support both John and their three children. Once in a while, John considers getting a job, then insists that a side job would detract from the "Lord's work." His wife left him before he came to see me.

I actually assessed John's chakra gift intuitively; he would have shouted "witchcraft!" at the thought that invisible little energy centers might have been planted within him. I theorized that John had a strong first chakra Manifesting gift in a secondary position. Over time, I helped John see the importance of living all of his values, such as providing for his family. He remembered a childhood interest in building and signed up to be an apprentice carpenter in a friend's business. Over time, John proved to his wife and to himself he could bring home the bacon, not just serve up the Bible, and his wife is now giving him a second chance.

As with solitary chakra types, John displayed the hearty strengths and weaknesses of his type. By arousing a secondary gift, he could counterbalance his Spiritualist aversion to sacrificing for the world and actually become a more fully spiritual person.

Lucy is an acquaintance who always knew that she wanted to be a counselor. Strong in the second chakra, Lucy feels everyone's feelings as if they are her own. A college major in social work did the trick, and Lucy became a parole officer.

Fast forward ten years, and we find a saddened, overweight, and depressed woman who can't stand going to work. Lucy can't cope with her natural tendency to absorb everyone's emotions. After sponging depression all day, she had no energy for play, relationships, or exercise. She ate and got more and more depressed. Lucy took one of my chakra gift-order tests. I wasn't surprised. She scored 30 on the second chakra, her next gifts, much lower.

Lucy did have a fairly strong tenth chakra, however. Her home already depicted the heart of a Naturalist. An old home on the historical register, it was constructed with wood and brick. She still cooked over a black-topped stove! And Lucy did cook. She loved to cook. After figuring out her bottom-line financial needs, Lucy partnered with a friend and began an evening catering business. She started slowly, using word of mouth to begin the business. Within two years, Lucy was able to take out a small business loan and update her kitchen to meet legal requirements. She now works part-time doing counseling for battered women and almost full-time at catering. She loves what she's doing and has a battery of new friends, plus a new wardrobe for a size-8 instead of a size-16 figure.

Both John and Lucy had to make changes in their lives. John's presenting problems were financial in nature and needed to be solved with practical, moneymaking strategies. Lucy's issues concerned her working life and energy. Her entire life benefited when she looked at other ways of making money. Both individuals were able to retain their authentic nature and, by reframing their sense of self and money, use their innate moneymaking styles to turn their lives around.

CONFIGURATION TWO:
IF YOU HAVE TWO STRONG CHAKRAS

The upside of having two strong chakras is that you can so easily make money at one skill area if the other is currently impractical. The problem is that you can feel torn between worlds or gifts and think that you have to choose.

Martha is a perfect example of a two-chakra person. Martha loves accounting. She really does. A strong third chakra Thinker, Martha could spend all day balancing books. She'd probably even tip them out of balance if she thought she could then work a little longer and harder. But Martha also likes art. She is a closet artist; in fact, during her college heyday, she majored in fine arts and spent years perfecting her sculpting skills. She's never been able to see how her day job can integrate her inner creative passion.

When asked what she'd like to do, Martha, very thoughtfully replied, "Well, that doesn't matter. I have expenses. I have to be an accountant!" Thinkers think fiscally in numbers and columns. Artists don't make money, so art won't feed the accounts receivables. Therefore to a Thinker, art is a waste of time. Except that Martha enjoyed her art and was good at it. Martha and I worked from a Thinker's money style, since that was her most developed monetary style. Using a financial consultant, Martha figured out what she really needed to make ends meet and spent a year paying off debt to cut her expenses further. She then gradually integrated more of her Feeler's creative personality and began taking accounting clients as a side business. She found that she liked working one-on-one with people, a Feeler trait, and was enthusiastic to switch to her own business when the money flow could sustain her basic needs. She had already budgeted art supplies in her financial plan and escrowed thousands of dollars for her creative work. It was therefore simple to convert this money into art equipment and begin to experiment artistically. Martha is now selling her sculptures in three antique stores, having developed a particular style that reproduces an ancient look.

Denny's two-chakra style actually helped rescue him from a financial dilemma. Denny was both a fifth chakra Communicator and a fourth chakra Relater. He worked as an employee assistance counselor at a large corporation, using his obvious interest in relationships to communicate problem-solving methods to employees. Work was working, but his personal life wasn't.

Relationships were number one to Denny. Unfortunately, his loyalty was costing him. His wife was a compulsive gambler. Because he didn't want to hurt her feelings or destroy the marriage, he continually forgave her. She flitted from therapist to therapist, but never changed. Married, Denny was financially responsible for her debts and he was drowning in them.

But was he telling anyone what was going on? Getting any support for himself? Denny needed to "work his own program." He did, first by reading literature about gambling and codependency, then by talking with experts about what to do. He finally hired a financial consultant to get real about the facts and how to protect his own assets. These actions used his communication skills and aptitude, which helped him when he initiated a legal separation to gain financial security.

Like Martha and Denny, two-chakra individuals can learn how to pull strengths from both chakras. While one skill-base can serve as secondary, it's smarter to use both in balance.

CONFIGURATION THREE:
IF YOU HAVE THREE STRONG CHAKRAS

Three-chakra individuals have multiple strengths. Sometimes the pull between the three can cause inner havoc, sometimes supreme blessings.

Picture your three strengths in triangle form. All three assets are available to you at all times, but you need to balance them by finding your base. What's the "bottom line?" What's the job title, character description or worldly label that best describes you or that works best in the world?

Maybe you're a tenth, second, and third chakra person. You like working with land, you care about others' feelings, and you're good at organizing. You've also got your real estate and mortgage broker licenses and a nonlicensed certificate in counseling from your synagogue. How do you add this together?

If you select the tenth chakra, you could describe yourself as a real estate agent that can issue mortgages and advertise yourself as the "full service agent who cares." If you go with the second chakra, you could set up a business as a housing counselor, offering an intake process to determine individuals' home and home-related financial needs. Individuals could then hire you for your other services depending upon the intake outcome. If you highlight your third chakra, you could call yourself a mortgage banker but tell your friends you'd be happy to get them a great real estate deal. The basic idea behind having three strong gifts is to figure out how to best arrange them.

A three-chakra person who comes to mind is Shana, an African woman who moved to New York a few years ago. Shana was an eighth chakra Shaman, an eleventh chakra Commander, and a sixth chakra Visionary. While these words would be new to her, she would recognize their descriptions.

Shana was raised in a tribe in Ghana, her grandmother teaching her about natural and spiritual forces as well as various means of psychically visioning others' physical illnesses. Shana was chosen to be her tribe's next shaman when AIDS just about wiped out her people. She and her brother were sent to the United States by a government agency. A congressman took special interest in them as did a church, and they were issued green cards. If they could find work, they could stay.

With no English, Shana enrolled in special tutoring classes. Work was another issue. What was she to do? An astute woman in the sponsoring church noticed Shana's healing gifts and encouraged Shana to join the prayer team. People changed. They healed. Over time, Shana put prayer and shamanism together and started her own healing business. With others' help, she actually began to introduce herself as a shaman. The exotic nature of the word actually increased her business, and her other abilities were easily described within the one label.

After running her business successfully, Shana hit another snag. She didn't really know how to manage or invest money. Think of it. Not a lot of real practical financial skills in the eighth or eleventh chakra! She did hold an untapped resource in her sixth chakra Visionary, however.

Shana and I worked to build a long-range financial plan, using Shana's clairvoyant abilities as a base and research organ. Basically, Shana pictured her long-range goals, including where she wanted to live, by when and how. We then went backward in time to construct a plan, including how much she should charge on an hourly rate and when to change her rates. We used a financial consultant to figure out Shana's taxes and other expenditures as well as critical investment vehicles, with Shana verifying each recommendation using her inner vision. Finally, Shana was presented a simple and clear plan that told her how many clients to see each week at what charge and what percentage of monies to save in which investment pool. Now the walker of all worlds could gainfully play in this one.

Can you see how a three-chakra person can use all skills, just in various orders?

CONFIGURATION FOUR:
IF YOU HAVE FOUR STRONG CHAKRAS

Wow! This can be a hard image to capture—and an even more challenging way to live! You're a generalist, not because you lack gifts and skills, but because you have so many.

As I said earlier, four-chakra people must, must, must get organized. Then, do as the three-chakra individual does. Pick a horse and put everything in the cart. Or, expand your worldview and package yourself as a generalist within a certain niche market. Think of your gifts as needing to be established in a square or a rectangle format, and you'll grasp the sort of stability you need to acquire. Let me give you an example of a "four star" that worked it out on his own.

Timothy is a highly gifted and talented individual who as a boy got straight A's in just about everything except, to his chagrin, maybe baseball. He graduated from high school at age 16 and went on to college.

He'd always loved animals and the sciences, so he decided to be a veterinarian. Here we see a strong fourth and third chakra gifting, with inclinations toward healing and systems. Timothy finished the eight-year program in five years and was suddenly confused. He didn't want to work with animals! He felt like that would be limiting his skills. So he took a computer course, a good Thinker skill, and developed a large-animal farm-management program, which hit it big internationally. Suddenly, Timothy was in demand worldwide as a teacher and speaker.

Timothy's fifth chakra abilities as a Communicator exploded. He loved the attention and the extra money. His connection into the world of people now caused a further problem, however. He found himself enjoying the various cultures he visited and the interpersonal associations between himself and others. Timothy's second chakra Feeler had expanded. He now decided he should chuck his previous profession and become either a therapist or an art and music dealer.

Fortunately, Timothy ran out of strong chakras at about this time, or he might have considered joining a monastery as a Spiritualist. Without knowing what to do, Timothy struck gold by quitting his professorial job and starting his own international consulting business. Simply calling himself a "Knowledge Expert," he balanced his abilities atop his strengths as a Thinker and Communicator and started subsidiaries within his own company. Knowledge Experts Unlimited now has an import-export cross-cultural art division, an agricultural development subsidiary, and a free counseling service to help nonprofit organizations develop profitable businesses for fourth-world countries.

If you, like Timothy and thousands of others, are a four-chakra person, know that time is on your side. You may not immediately be able to capitalize on your aptitudes, but time will bring you more opportunities. Stay creative and think creatively.

CONFIGURATION FIVE:
IF YOU HAVE MORE THAN FOUR STRONG CHAKRAS

Falling apart yet? Feel like you're so good at so many things that you're not good at anything? Your money is probably in an equally blundering mess. Unless you can sort out your gifts, you'll have a hard time sorting your money.

Start with boundaries. Insert boundaries and live every day within boundaries. Let me give you an example.

Markus was gifted in six chakras, all of equal strength. Even his so called lower ones weren't very low scoring. The only weak chakra was his sixth, which totaled 10 out of 30 points. Markus was so environmentally sensitive, he couldn't work in most work settings without sneezing all the time. He was so Feeling he couldn't be around negative people. Even though he was a Spiritualist and a Relater, he couldn't tolerate others' pain and suffering. As a Manifester, he was actually absorbing others' pain and illnesses into his own body, which didn't leave much time for his incredibly high IQ and Thinker abilities to act very profoundly. A voracious reader and musician, Markus's Communicator abilities were just about all that kept him going. Fortunately, his communication assets were supported by his Spiritualist and Idealist tendencies to appreciate the finer things in life. Life would have been good except that sitting around and listening to religious CDs while reading the classics doesn't pay the bills. Markus's bill collectors knew him by name, though none thought they could collect on an individual whose highest paying job was selling shoes at JC Penney, a large American department store chain.

Markus and I talked a lot about psychic boundaries, means of screening incoming intuitive information for your own well-being. These techniques kept Markus from being victimized by his own gifts until he began to gain a sense of self and self-esteem. You know what I then recommended? I suggested that Markus throw his weight behind his weakest chakra, the sixth chakra, and actually become a corporate Visionary. We cleaned up his attire, and I had Markus cut a "Creative Ideation" CD, full of his ideas about the world and needed products. He analyzed various marketplaces and global situations that could provide inspirational products for business and would be advantaged in return. He then sent this CD with marketing materials to several corporations.

He waited. Then he got a call. "Do you do brainstorming focus groups?" the marketing director asked. Now, Markus wasn't yet ready for groups, so I suggested that he be honest and say no. Instead, I prompted Markus to offer a free research audit via phone interviews and material assessments. Markus could then submit recommendations, and if the company liked them, they could hire him on retainer to provide creative ideas. They bought it. Markus was a great success. And he's now on retainer with four major corporations. They call him the "idea man." Only a few of his clients have even met him, which adds to his mystique as a Visionary. Markus now has money. His natural aptitudes enable him to invest independently. Frankly, he makes more now in the stock market than through his business.

If you have a lot of strong chakras, I suggest that you get help with boundaries and career development if your life is confusing and your money even more so.

CONFIGURATION SIX:
IF YOUR CHAKRAS ARE MAINLY IN THE MIDRANGE

Do you ever feel like you have no true abilities or gifts? Maybe my test doesn't work for you. Interview friends and examine your past to figure your true gifts. Consult with a career-development or placement service and take formal tests, for that matter.

The other possibility is that for some reason, you're hiding your light in the dark. Sometimes families discourage rather than encourage a child's natural expression. If your family is full of doctors and you're artistic, or worse, shamanic, they might squelch your abilities. You might feel so odd that you assume there's no place for you in the world. Perhaps you have locked your gift into a closet and there it sits.

Marcia had secreted her abilities into a small corner in her heart, probably because they were so unacceptable to her family. Marcia came to me because she felt like she wasn't getting anywhere in life. She made a living but never enough money to go anywhere or do anything. At age 40, she had practically no savings and no real promotional opportunities.

In working with Marcia, I determined that she was a fifth chakra Communicator but on the more esoteric level. She heard words in her head. When she was a child, she heard the voices of God and angels, the dead and the invisible. Her mother suggested that Marcia was crazy and submitted her to a round of examinations by psychologists intent on identifying psychoses. All confirmed that Marcia was indeed crazy. Given the choice of being crazy or normal, Marcia chose the latter and never, never heard voices again.

I first theorized Marcia's true gifts by looking at her life. In every way, Marcia displayed Communicator attributes. She loved to read and listen to music. She avidly wrote in her journal and worked a help line in a bank. So why didn't she test as a Communicator on any of my tests?

When Marcia shared her real story, the answer became apparent. I asked Marcia if she would like to further develop her gift, and she said yes, if it could be done safely. She took classes with me and at her church and learned to hear her own inner wisdom and God's guidance. And her writing gift exploded.

I encouraged Marcia to write for publication, which she did. She reported that the "words flow through her," making her job easier. She simply listens and writes. This was a year ago. While Marcia is still holding onto her day job, she's making a few hundred dollars extra a month on her writing. She's investing this money in order to buy a house and is also exploring getting tuition reimbursement for training in editing for the bank.

It's okay to be in the middle range and it's also okay to realize that you might have secreted a strong gift in a closet. If you have a lot of midrange chakras, do what's necessary to support your searching process. You deserve it.

CONFIGURATION SEVEN:
IF YOU HAVE A LOT OF WEAK CHAKRAS

Don't be scared if most of your chakras are weak. Weak is such a judgmental word, isn't it? Our world discredits lack and limitation. We are all fragile in some areas. Why would we want to be vibrant and exposed in every area of our lives? As long as you have one strong gift, you can access your spiritual nature and move through the world with grace. Weaknesses often force us to follow our strengths.

If you feel bad about having weak chakras, consider that the meaning of the word "weak" is vulnerable and fragile. It might be that exposing your gifts could leave you vulnerable, and so you dilute your natural gifts to remain safe. If you've tested low and it doesn't feel right, consider examining your past or current reality for reasons causing low self-esteem. You might be deliberately secreting your gifts.

I think of one client in particular. Jordan was a middle-aged woman living with an abusive husband. She tested low in all the chakras. Daily, Jordan was subjected to insults, shaming comments, and nasty treatment. Her husband didn't hit her. He never gave her a reason to call the police. Instead, he told her she was too fat, ugly, and demonic for him to find interesting or sexy. He mocked her work, although she made more money than he did. Ironically, Jordan was extremely petite, gifted, and lively. Her low chakra scores reflected the intense put-downs. Her scores rose after she left her husband—as did her income!

No matter what your test scores are, your truest gift lies within your heart. It is your heart! It is the way you examine and grow from experience your bravery and courage in meeting life's challenges and the means you use to meet your end goals. No matter how you look at it, money is really just a means to an end. The end is expansion of your true nature, through both the easy and the difficult times. It is the light that shines in the dark.

But as it is said: a light in the dark must share its light or it becomes a shadow. Make money. Manage it well. And remember always to bless others with the blessings you've earned.

An Exercise in Money Making and Management

Part One: Owning Your Style

In the margins of this page, please list your top-scoring chakras and their titles. Then complete these questions for each chakra by inserting the titles of your strongest chakras in each blank. Note: You will fill out parts one through four for each of your strongest or weakest chakras. For instance, if you have three strong chakras, then in part one you will fill out questions one through five for each of these chakras. Do the same with parts one through four.

1. I am a _____ (title of the chakra, such as Manifester or Feeler), in these ways:

2. My greatest asset as a _____ is that I am this way:

3. I express my spiritual nature as a _____ in that I do the following:

4. I deal with money as a _____ in that I believe and do the following:

5. If I had all the money in the world, as a _____
I would do the following:

Part Two: Getting Honest

1. As a _____, I could have been better at the
following:

2. When acting as a _____, I made these
mistakes:

3. When making money as a _____, I failed to
use these character assets:

4. When making or spending money as a _____,
I hurt myself or others this way:

5. When saving or managing money as a _____,
I made these mistakes:

Part Three: Setting Goals

1. As a _____, I really want to accomplish the
following while alive:

2. As a _____, I need money because it provides
me with this:

3. As a _____, I really want to use these means
to make money:

4. As a _____, I want to manage or save my
money using the following means:

5. As a _____, I want to leave this financial legacy
when dead:

Part Four: Implementing Change

1. As a _____, I can draw on these gifts or strengths to make money:

2. As a _____, I must avoid these tendencies so I can be financially responsible:

3. As a _____, I need to get the following assistance in order to be effective:

4. Lacking the gifts of _____ (insert your weakest chakras), I need to obtain the following assistance to be affective:

5. The characteristics of my supportive chakra, _____, will help me do the following:

Part Five: Unifying Yourself

1. The single word that best describes my combined strengths is this:

2. The single phrase that best explains my spiritual nature is this:

3. The single phrase that best depicts my professional purpose is this:

4. The single phrase that best characterizes my purpose in relationships is this:

5. The single phrase that best clarifies my personality is this:

6. When added together, my moneymaking strengths include:

7. When added together, my money management strengths include:

8. When added together, it seems that the best ways for me to make money are to:

9. When added together, it seems the best ways to manage and save my money are to:

10. In summation, my moneymaking and management style can best be described this way:

6

Applications in Moneymaking:
The Four Ways to Energize Prosperity

"Generosity, in fact, was one of the cardinal virtues that all Lakota men strove to cultivate and practice. The measure of achievement in these virtues determined the tangible wealth . . . and the reputation and influence enjoyed in the band or tribe. Inculcated from early childhood, the four virtues were bravery, fortitude, generosity, and wisdom."[8]

Taking your strengths, there are four steps ruling how to make money:

1. Physical effort
2. Emotional manifesting
3. Mental beliefs
4. Spiritual mission

Through your chakra gifts, you can apply any of these means for encouraging abundance and prosperity. You'll need to use them all at some point, but only you can decide if you're willing to put the effort into the last type of moneymaking, the spiritualization of pure energy.

PHYSICAL EFFORT

Ninety-five percent of us operate on the effort level 95 percent of the time. "Efforting" means that if we put in X amount of energy, we will reap X amount of benefit. A Manifester shows effort by getting cement and water and laying a driveway for a client. An Idealist efforts by joining a save the whales group and picketing on the beach. A Feeler-Artist will pay debt by selling her backlogged art at a craft fair. Efforting works only if you stay within your strengths because otherwise you're working against your own energy.

Positive Side of Efforting
Efforting produces strength of character, ability to persevere, and gratitude for outcome. It can also result in true success! Exertion is necessary for any change in the physical world. You must be willing to put in energy to receive something back. You must have "fortitude," one of the four cardinal virtues of the Lakota. The question is, what kind of energy do you want to spend and how much do you have?

Negative Side of Efforting
A lot of people start a career, a job, or a debt repayment program and quit because effort takes so much energy. If they don't

substitute another form of moneymaking, they fail financially. Other individuals aren't willing to pay the cost. To effort in one area of your life, you have to pull energy from another life area.

When efforting, you need to put in X amount of time to achieve success. X can equal time with family, friends, self, or spiritual pursuits. Some money types are more willing to pay the cost than others, such as Manifesters, Thinkers, Communicators, Visionaries, and ironically, certain value-driven Spiritualists and Idealists. And what are they losing for the exertion?

Here's the quandary of efforting. If you don't try, you sacrifice your spiritual destiny and end up disappointed in yourself. If you try too hard, you sacrifice balance.

EMOTIONAL MANIFESTING

People searching for an easier way than efforting move to the emotional level.

"Emotion" actually means "E-Mote," or ENERGY in MOTION. Emotions get us going and can keep us going. They make life colorful, allow connections between ourselves and other people and keep us honest.

The basis of all emotions are feelings. Humanity shares the same basic five "feeling constellations," which are feeling groups that describe all the known feelings. An emotion is actually a belief joined with at least one feeling. The belief tells us what to do, and the feeling provides us the raw energy to get going.

The five basic feeling constellations are joy, fear, anger, sadness, and disgust. Joy tells us to keep doing what we're doing while fear warns us of danger, insisting that we move forward or backward. Anger informs us that our boundaries have been violated; sometimes we get angry because we've violated our own inner self. Sadness encourages us to look underneath a loss for the love causing us to grieve. Disgust is a natural and instinctual urge to purge, to get rid of something or someone toxic to us. Shame is a version of disgust, informing us that someone else is trying to make us wrong. Guilt is a form of self-disgust, telling us we're doing something regretful.

Emotional manifesting occurs when our feelings play one of these two parts in manifesting or in refusing to manifest:

1. The motivating reason.
2. The motivating energy.

People often manifest or refuse to manifest because of emotional reasons. These rationales can be specific to each chakra type.

Some very financially successful people manifest out of emotions. Consider a Manifester who is afraid of being poor because her father was a failure. Her fear might drive her to the top of the earnings chart! A Relater might drive himself into riches because otherwise, he'd feel guilty at not providing for his family. Consider the Feeler who works hard because success makes him feel joyful or happy.

People also have emotional reasons for failing—even failing to try! For instance, a Manifester might feel guilty about succeeding when his failure of a father didn't succeed. While one Feeler feels happy being prosperous, another might be embarrassed about her life gifts and doesn't want to attract attention to herself. It's not uncommon to find Spiritualists who are angry at secular authority, such as the IRS, and are therefore unwilling to earn money that the "enemy" might steal. Clearly emotions can serve as the reason to become financially successful or not.

Emotions can encourage or inhibit success because feelings are tangible energies that carry information. Scientists, including Dr. Candace Pert, are clearly demonstrating that feelings are energetic in origin: in the body, different feelings are produced from different chemicals. Some successful individuals actually "pay" for their success with their emotional energy. They are able to channel anger into a drive for success or even into clear thinking.

Perhaps they are really angry at their failure of a dad, but they focus their anger for success. Yet other angry people can use the emotional energy to build a wall around themselves and prevent abundance. All emotions carry information that creates success or failure.

Different chakra types tend to use different feelings to get their needs met. Based on my experience, the various chakra types manifest with these feelings:

- *Emotional Manifesting: First Chakra Manifester*
  Shame, disgust, guilt, terror, anger, hurt, rage, sadness, abandonment, hunger, joy, satisfaction.

- *Emotional Manifesting: Second Chakra Feeler*
  Sadness, anger, happiness, fear, closeness, reassurance, comfort, mergence, expansion.

- *Emotional Manifesting: Third Chakra Thinker*
  Specific fears and judgments, exhaustion, disgust, recognition, revenge, rewards, sweetness, knowing.

- *Emotional Manifesting: Fourth Chakra Relater*
  Happiness, closeness, compassion, loneliness, alienation, despair, sorrow, grief, terror, rejection, abandonment, hurt, emptiness, rage, anger.

- *Emotional Manifesting: Fifth Chakra Communicator*
  Understanding, connection, acceptance, repression, violation, expression, fear, duty, disgust, sadness.

- *Emotional Manifesting: Sixth Chakra Visionary*
  Achievement, importance, prevention, fear of danger, disenchantment, incorrectness (righting wrongs), clarity, self-hatred, self-acceptance.

- *Emotional Manifesting: Seventh Chakra Spiritualist*
  Shame, self-guilt, community guilt, rage at self or oth-

ers, disappointment, devaluation, joy at service, spiritual closeness, spiritual rewards or recognition, justice or injustice, fear of failure, fear of success.

- *Emotional Manifesting: Eighth Chakra Shaman*
  Powerfulness, disempowerment, curiosity, revenge, renewal, delight, antagonism, wretchedness, freedom, containment, self-sacrifice, awareness.

- *Emotional Manifesting: Ninth Chakra Idealist*
  Revolution, union, sharing, romanticism, optimism, connection, dissatisfaction, pride, arrogance, anger, bitterness.

- *Emotional Manifesting: Tenth Chakra Naturalist*
  Groundedness, goodness, closeness, empathetic sadness, anger at wrongness, powerlessness, attachment, connection, tranquility.

- *Emotional Manifesting: Eleventh Chakra Commander*
  Powerfulness, bliss, righteousness, resentment, forcefulness, surrender, confinement, correctness, servanthood.

Positive Side of Emotional Manifesting

Emotions are simply discharged energies. We all have emotions and we will always create new emotions. You can learn how to transform any emotion into a motivator. Feeling shameful and bad about yourself? Why let it get you stuck? Use emotional "bravery," one of the four cardinal Lakota virtues. Own your faults; you can even read your chakra style to pinpoint your weak spots. Then transform your negativity into a goal, an endeavor, even a reason to learn forgiveness and self-acceptance. Unconditional love is only a "yes" away. No matter how spiritual we become, we will always use emotions when manifesting. The key is that we don't want our motivation to be emotional. We can learn to foster emotions that keep us in motion—while refusing to be motivated by emotions.

Negative Side of Emotional Manifesting

Using emotions as your primary motivation or investment energy creates continual tension in your body and in your life. You can become dependent upon a certain emotion or set of emotions to create or maintain a "set point" of success.

A set point is your acceptable level of success. Less than a certain point and you don't feel safe. More than a certain point, you don't feel secure. Emotional motivation can keep you stuck at a certain place. That makes it hard to excel any further than where you are—and also guarantees that you'll slip to your lower setpoint if you ever do achieve success!

Using emotional energy as the primary means of achievement will backfire. Maybe anger, for example, will help a savvy person create a financially secure business. When directed into a marriage, anger is sure to inhibit closeness or intimacy! Any long-held emotion will create emotional patterns, habitual emotional reactions to external events or internal needs. Your emotions can then control you instead of the other way around.

MENTAL BELIEFS

Beliefs underlie almost all human actions. Some successful people succeed because they believe it is their right to do so; others because they believe that unless they succeed, they are bad people. Some people don't succeed because they don't believe that they deserve success; others because they believe that money is evil. If they make money, they are then evil.

After playing in the playground of feelings, most of us examine the role that the mind or belief systems occupy in our manifestation abilities. The truth is, beliefs are significant in both efforting and emotional manifesting anyway. Efforting is based upon the belief that X produces Y. Emotional manifesting joins feelings with beliefs; feelings empower the desire of the belief. Manifesting through beliefs alone keeps the feeling and physical labor out of the process so you can think and plan better.

There are six primary types of beliefs. These are all dualist, meaning we tend to believe either the positive or negative side of these six beliefs.

Primary Belief	Negative Aspect	Positive Aspect
Worthiness	I am unworthy	I am worthy
Deserving	I don't deserve	I do deserve
Power	I am powerless	I am powerful
Value	I have no value	I am valuable
Love	I am not loveable	I am loveable
Goodness	I am bad (or evil)	I am good

Everybody is affected by these beliefs. And everyone has at least one belief in the negative.

What? It would seem that successful people must have only positive beliefs. Guess again. Some successful people manifest money because they don't think they are worthy! Believing themselves inherently unlovable, for instance, they might earn money as a way of earning approval. Yet other successful individuals might believe themselves to have no value. For them, having money is a way to prove value.

It's easy to see how unsuccessful people are ruled by their negative beliefs. If I don't deserve abundance, I won't make a decent living. Look in the shadows and you find people refusing success, however, because they twist the positive belief into a pretzel.

For instance, some individuals might decide that because they are valuable, they are "too good" to worry about making money! Consequently, they might cost a lot of other people a lot of money, living on the welfare system when they could be working—or continuing to live at home long past their adult due dates. Someone like this might really be avoiding the real issue, a negative belief like "I am powerless." He or she might simply be too scared to try to succeed, believing himself or herself too weak to achieve any real recognition or to stand up to resistance.

The various chakra types tend to concentrate on different negative or positive beliefs. I've covered a few of these in the individual chakra descriptions. Here is a brief recap:

Potential Core Beliefs: First Chakra Manifester

Worthiness	I am worthy or unworthy of having my needs met.
Deserving	I do or do not deserve to have my needs met.
Power	I am able or not able to get my needs met.
Value	I am valued or have no value in the physical world.
Love	I am loveable or not loveable in primary relationships.
Goodness	My body is good or bad.

Potential Core Beliefs: Second Chakra Feeler

Worthiness	I am worthy or unworthy of being accepted.
Deserving	I do or do not deserve to express my feelings.
Power	I am powerful or not powerful enough to express my feelings.
Value	My feelings are valued or not valued.
Love	I am loveable or not loveable, no matter how I feel.
Goodness	My feelings are good or bad.

Potential Core Beliefs: Third Chakra Thinker

Worthiness	I am worthy or unworthy of being rewarded for what I achieve.
Deserving	I do or do not deserve to be recognized for my thoughts.
Power	I have or do not have enough power to make a difference.
Value	My work is valued or not valuable.

| Love | I am loveable or not loveable, no matter how I act. |
| Goodness | My thoughts are good or they are bad. |

Potential Core Beliefs: Fourth Chakra Relater

Worthiness	I am worthy or unworthy of being unconditionally loved.
Deserving	I deserve or don't deserve loving relationships.
Power	Love is powerful enough or powerless to heal others and me.
Value	As I am, I have value or no value in relationships.
Love	I am loveable or I am not loveable, just as I am.
Goodness	I am good or I am bad (or evil).

Potential Core Beliefs: Fifth Chakra Communicator

Worthiness	I am worthy or unworthy of being heard.
Deserving	I deserve or don't deserve to express my truth.
Power	I am powerful enough or powerless to express my truth
Value	My views are valuable or not valuable.
Love	I am loved or not loved when I fully express myself.
Goodness	My views are good or bad.

Potential Core Beliefs: Sixth Chakra Visionary

Worthiness	I am worthy or not worthy of succeeding at my goals.
Deserving	I deserve or don't deserve a fruitful life path.
Power	As I am, I have enough or not enough power to reach my goals.
Value	I see myself as a valuable or not valuable person.
Love	I see myself as loveable or not loveable.
Goodness	I am innately good or bad.

Potential Core Beliefs: Seventh Chakra Spiritualist

| Worthiness | I am worthy or unworthy of God's love. |
| Deserving | I deserve or don't deserve God's love. |

Power	Good is more powerful than evil, or evil is stronger than good.
Value	I know myself as valued or not valued by God.
Love	As a human being, I am loveable or not loveable to God.
Goodness	I am good or I am evil.

Potential Core Beliefs: Eighth Chakra Shaman

Worthiness	I am worthy or unworthy of my abilities.
Deserving	I deserve or don't deserve respect from others.
Power	I have powers or no powers.
Value	My gifts are valuable or not valuable to the world.
Love	I am loveable or not loveable no matter how I perform.
Goodness	I am an agent of good or an agent of evil.

Potential Core Beliefs: Ninth Chakra Idealist

Worthiness	The world is worthy or not worthy of my help.
Deserving	I deserve or don't deserve to be accepted with imperfections.
Power	I am powerful or not powerful enough to make a difference.
Value	I am valued or not valued for how I serve.
Love	I am loveable or not loveable, despite my imperfections.
Goodness	The world is good or the world is bad.

Potential Core Beliefs: Tenth Chakra Naturalist

Worthiness	I am worthy or not worthy of being alive.
Deserving	I deserve or don't deserve a happy life.
Power	I have all the power I need or not to live a constructive life.
Value	I have value in my family (or on this planet) or I do not.
Love	I am loveable or not loveable in my natural state.
Goodness	Nature is good or it must be subdued.

Potential Core Beliefs: Eleventh Chakra Commander

Worthiness   I am worthy or not worthy of my powers

Deserving   I deserve or don't deserve to own my powers.

Power   I am powerful or I am powerless.

Value   I have value or no value, no matter what I accomplish.

Love   I am loveable or I am not loveable.

Goodness   I am good or I am bad (or evil).

Positive Side of Belief-Based Manifesting

Manifesting through beliefs is very powerful. Basically, you can manifest what you believe that you deserve to manifest. Change just one belief and your life immediately reflects this change.

The key to belief-based manifesting is to stop looking for outcome. Just start believing the positive; start by considering that a half-full glass is better than a half-empty glass. Don't try to add more to the glass. If you begin with appreciating what you have, you will naturally attract more—without the cost of efforting or emoting. Your new thinking will produce better thoughts. You will learn "generosity," one of the four cardinal virtues of the Lakota. The increased clarity will help you form better decisions and therefore more success.

Negative Side of Belief-Based Manifesting

Beliefs are like trees. A single negative belief branches into dozens and eventually thousands of other negative beliefs. It's difficult to unearth the beliefs affecting our growth and success. The mind is very complicated and so is the process necessary to change our mindsets, or belief-based set points. Trying to achieve success solely by telling yourself that you are worthy or deserving is a long if not impossible process.

SPIRITUAL MISSION

We all have a spirit. Your spirit is that unique and special part of you that reflects the Divine.

You are Divine. In the Bible, this idea is introduced in Genesis, which reveals that we are all created in God's image—male and female. Most of us identify with being either feminine or masculine without recognizing that this story in Genesis contains the key to natural abundance: we are all invested with the Spirit—and the Spirit is a creative spirit.

Through creative energy, the Divine manufactured the natural and spiritual forces necessary to manufacture, imprint, and continue creating the physical universe. Natural forces include scientifically evidenced laws like gravity and the existence of electricity. Spiritual forces are those that motivate and energize the spiritual gifts and include broad-ranging powers like creativity, abundance, harmony, and faith. Because our spirits are made from the greater Spirit, we can marshal the spiritual forces as well as the natural ones. In fact, the Divine desires that we use all resources at our disposal to create more heaven on earth.

When we manifest by following our spiritual mission, we are provided the gift of spiritual power. We are able to call upon the spiritual forces that the Spirit used to create the universe. We can summon the energies needed to help others—as we are designed to do. If you are a Manifester, you have divine right to summon the natural and spiritual forces necessary to make money, build an empire, or provide for a family. If you are an Idealist, you are divinely seeded with the skills and abilities to connect people around important ideals and goals.

As you accept and pursue your spiritual mission, you become even more aware of the presence of the Divine in everyday life. Even the small tasks in life become easier. Do you need the freshest head of lettuce for a party? The Divine is present in the great and the small. By all means, access Divine wisdom for your cooking project. Who knows if a job offer might come out of the event?

The Divine's job is to recognize, support, and guide you. Your job is to figure out your divine mission and to access the energy you need to fulfill it.

While reading this book, I hope you've come closer to knowing your spiritual mission and divine gifts. Following your true essence will energize your life. It will also energize money—as well as all your other needs—to you. Love is a principle and an action. If you follow the truths invested in you, the universe will respond lovingly. Consider again the four cardinal virtues mentioned at the beginning of this chapter: bravery, fortitude, generosity, and wisdom. Seeing your true self is a courageous act; living this self no matter what takes fortitude. Giving freely from this self is a generous expression of spirit. And as you reveal your wisdom to the world, you will prosper.

Notes

1. Williams, Niall, *The Fall of Light* (New York: Warner Books, 2001), p. 155.
2. Smith, Huston, *The Religions of Man* (New York: Harper & Row, 1958), p. 199.
3. Smith, *The Religions of Man,* p. 45.
4. Ywahoo, Dhyani, *Voices of Our Ancestors* (Boston: Shambhala Publications, 1987), p. 191.
5. Attanasio, A. A., *The Serpent and the Grail* (New York: HarperCollins, 1999), p. 189.
6. Lee, Tanith, *Red Unicorn* (New York: Tom Doherty, 1997), p. 180.
7. Nolan, Han, *Dancing on the Edge* (New York: Puffin Books, 1997), p. 243.
8. Utley, Robert, *The Lance and the Shield* (New York: Ballantine Books, 1993), p. 11.